*BOSTON AND THE
TEA RIOTS*

BOSTON AND THE TEA RIOTS

by NORMA R. FRYATT

AUERBACH
publishers

princeton
philadelphia
new york
london

Copyright © Norma R. Fryatt 1972

Published simultaneously in Canada by Book Center, Inc.

Library of Congress Catalog Card Number: 77-178036
International Standard Book Number: 0-87769-114-2

First Printing

Printed in the United States of America

With appreciation
to B. W. L., R. P. R., and D. C.
who helped

Contents

	List of Illustrations	ix
1.	Raising a Revenue	1
2.	Bonfire A-Building	17
3.	Thomas Hutchinson: Born and Educated Among Us	25
4.	Boston Under Pressure	33
5.	The Ships, the Body Meetings, and the Laws	47
6.	Boston Harbor a Teapot	55
7.	Aftermath	63
8.	How the News Was Received in London	77
9.	Lord North	83
10.	Riots and Proceedings	87
11.	Measures Against Boston	91
12.	Will Boston Submit?	97
13.	Condemned Without a Hearing	103
14.	A Congress Meets	113
	Appendix I	123
	Appendix II	127
	Appendix III	133
	Notes	137
	Reading List	143
	Index	145

List of Illustrations

Facsimile autograph of James Otis	9
The Hutchinson house on Garden Court, Boston	26
Thomas Hutchinson's personal seal	31
Design from the masthead of the *Boston Gazette*	33
The Liberty Tree as it looked in 1774	36
Column from the *Boston Gazette* of December 20, 1773	45
Destruction of the tea in Boston Harbor, December 16, 1773	58
Letter from Admiral Montagu, December 16, 1773	64
TEA Destroyed by Indians	70
Lord North	84
Threepenny piece of reign of George III	104
Carpenters' Hall, Philadelphia	118

1. *Raising a Revenue*

As the colonial governors repeatedly discovered, the people of the Massachusetts Bay Colony jealously guarded their rights. They had come to this wild new land, settled it, and cleared, sown, plowed, and harvested its fields. Every bit of their strength was invested in it. They had come to be free to live the kind of life they had been prevented from living in Europe. Now they were quick to detect and repel restraints on that freedom. As the first governor of Massachusetts, John Winthrop, had written in the 1640s, "We are bound to keep off whatsoever appears to tend to our ruin or damage."

To further that purpose, the colonists made it their business to find out about the law. As early as 1647 the people of Boston voted to procure for the town's use various English law books, among them Dalton's *Justice of the Peace* and Edward Coke's commentaries on Littleton and on the Magna Carta. By the 18th century young Americans were being sent to London's famous Inns of Court to study law. They returned to America to practice. Members of the Boston bar—Jeremiah Gridley, James Otis, and John Adams, for example—in the 1740s accumulated valuable libraries of law books on which to draw for authority in arguing their cases. They devoted long hours to the study of laws, principles of government, local charters, and the statutes and legal decisions that made up the British constitution.

Under Massachusetts' 1691 charter, the colony's government became more democratic than most of the other provincial governments in America. The main governing body, the General Court (also called the Assembly), consisted of the Crown-appointed governor and the elected legislature. The legislature had an upper house called the Council, composed of 28 popularly elected members, and a lower house, the House of Representatives, members of which were elected by the qualified voters of the colony. The governor was the only Crown appointee in the executive branch. His powers included the right to veto legislation and, if he saw fit, to reject members elected for the Council.

Any threat to this charter, which Massachusetts inhabitants considered the bastion of their liberties, caused their hackles to rise.

Recognizing that the law affected their lives and property, Americans had come to believe that they had a right to participate in the making of laws. Some did so through lively discussions in town meetings, through holding office as members of colonial legislatures, and through voting. Before the Revolutionary War, the vote in Massachusetts was given to adult male freeholders and to other adult male inhabitants with an estate worth £40 or an annual income of 40 shillings.

Since Boston was Massachusetts' seat of government and the abode of many of the colony's leading citizens and officials, Boston town meeting served as an exchange of views not only on town matters but also on larger issues, and sent its instructions to Boston's representatives in the Assembly. Opinions on the heart of the law itself—the natural rights of citizens—were debated in town meetings, where citizens did not hesitate to pass judgments on acts of Parliament and to seek ways to put those judgments into effect.

The acts of the British Parliament that most concerned the American colonies before 1764 were those that controlled colonial shipping. In essence, British policy tended to discourage colonial and foreign manufactures that competed with the products of Britain, but it also protected markets for such colonial products as fish, lumber, tobacco, rice, and sugar.

New England's prosperity at that time depended on the sea. The region's trade with the French and Spanish islands in the West Indies was especially important, for, unlike the Southern colonies, New England did not produce large staple crops. The shipyards supplied hundreds of colonial-built ships of all sizes to English merchants, and New England sea captains were kept busy trying all ports and risking almost any cargo for a profit.

During the Seven Years War (1756-1763), Americans, while aiding Britain militarily, persisted in trading with the West Indian islands. This greatly irritated the British because it profited the enemy (France) while Britain had been spending vast sums, she claimed, in defending America from the French and Indians. Since citizens of the home country were being heavily taxed to help pay for this defense, many Englishmen of high and low estate agreed that it was time the Americans paid a larger share. Was not the powerful British navy protecting colonial vessels and the home country providing a sure market for colonial produce?

Travelers returning to England from the American colonies reported on the prosperity there. The American merchants and their wives and children, "clothed gayly in fabrics of fantastic names from remote regions,"[1] could afford to have their portraits painted and to build handsome square mansions like those of English squires. If they could afford these, they could pay more toward the upkeep of the newly expanded British Empire.* One Englishman had figured that his countrymen were paying yearly taxes of 25 shillings per person while Americans were paying only six pence per person.

The first of a series of new revenue acts passed by Parliament was the Sugar Act of 1764, placing a direct tax on foreign molasses and sugar imported by the colonies. This act also provided for new and higher duties on non-British textiles, coffee, indigo, and Madeira and Canary wines. Lord Grenville, in charge of the Treasury at this time, determined that this tax measure would be enforced in America. Some of the customs officers there had become lazy and allowed themselves to be bribed, looking the other way when dutiable cargoes were slipped ashore at many inlets and harbors along the North Atlantic coast.

To this end, Grenville reformed the customs system and established a new vice-admiralty court at Halifax, Nova Scotia, where violators of the trade laws would be tried. Although the revenues from the Sugar Act were to be spent to defend, protect, and secure the American colonies, the colonists were not grateful. In fact they raised the major question of Parliament's right to levy taxes on Americans.

James Otis, a prominent Boston lawyer and member of the Massachusetts House of Representatives, was always ready to explain and expound his views on the law. He talked of *natural law*—a basic law or rule of right underlying all written or enacted law. He quoted the English philosopher

---

*By the Treaty of Paris this now included Canada, all of North America east of the Mississippi River and former French colonies in India.

John Locke whose doctrine on taxation held that if anyone shall claim a power to lay and levy taxes on the people without their consent, he thereby invades the fundamental law of property and subverts the end of government. This doctrine seemed entirely right to most Americans.

Such attitudes and ideas, however, were profoundly disturbing to the Crown-appointed governors of Massachusetts —men such as Francis Bernard and his successor, Thomas Hutchinson, who had sworn to abide by the decrees of King and Parliament. That "the plain people" have the right to pass judgment on governmental acts that affect them was sheer effrontery to Hutchinson.

The earliest official reaction to the Sugar Act came from Boston. The town's instructions to its representatives in the Massachusetts legislature on this matter, drafted and presented by Samuel Adams in May 1764, were a foretaste of things to come. Bostonians protested that such taxes were in restraint of trade and were illegal because the colonies were not represented in Parliament and had had no voice in passing the measure. Boston warned that more taxes would very likely be imposed if these were submitted to and suggested that the colonies present a united front in order to force Britain to change her policy.

In protest of the Sugar Act, James Otis, in 1764, published a pamphlet entitled *Rights of the British Colonies Asserted and Proved*. He declared that it was inherent in British law that "the supreme power cannot take from any man any part of his property, without his consent in person, or by representation; taxes are not to be laid on the people, but by their consent or by deputation." Otis then went on to state: "this right, if it could be traced no higher than Magna Carta, is part of the common law, part of a British subject's birthright, and as inherent and perpetual as the duty of Allegiance, both which have been brought to these colonies, and have been hitherto held sacred and inviolable." This pamphlet was read and discussed widely in the colonies, where mass meetings were being held to protest the Sugar Act and to urge nonimportation and nonexportation agreements in order to defeat it. Otis's pamphlet was also sent to the Massachusetts Bay Colony's agent in London and was published there.

Although some of the American colonies employed such agents to serve in London, the agents had no voice or vote in Parliament. The agent's role was to learn of any legislation that might affect the colony he represented, to seek to avert legislation harmful to it, and to canvass members of Parliament and ministers on behalf of his colony. Although not every colony had a London agent at any given time, many colonies eventually found it advisable to maintain one in London on a more or less regular basis. Nevertheless, an agent might be refused recognition by the British Government on a technicality, such as that he represented only the *lower house* of a colonial legislature and not the whole body. His position was equivocal at best.

While Americans were mounting their campaign against the Sugar Act, the British were planning to collect yet another tax as a source of revenue—a stamp tax. Under an act passed to become law on November 1, 1765, stamps costing from one halfpenny to £10 each would be required to be affixed to legal documents and records, newspapers, and even playing cards and dice. Also, the stamps would have to be paid for in *specie,* or hard cash, an item then scarce in the colonies.

To strengthen the customs authorities in America, the Lords of the Treasury sent soldiers and a naval contingent to the chief American ports. This met with particular opposition from colonists who felt that they did not need to bear the burden and expense of an enlarged military, naval, and customs establishment. Moreover, the impressment of Americans by the British navy that had been going on for years and the seizure of colonial ships suspected of carrying dutiable goods was also resented.

The remonstrances of the colonial agents did not prevent the passage of the Stamp Act. When the news of its passage reached America in May 1765, the voice of Patrick Henry rang out immediately in the Virginia House of Burgesses. A famous lawyer and a fiery orator, Henry introduced seven resolutions against the Stamp Act and gained passage of five of them by a close vote. The text of all seven was circulated through the other colonies. These Virginia resolutions, having been adopted by one of the most populous and the oldest of the British colonies, had an enormous influence, causing no less than eight other colonies to fall in line. Because of the clarity of their statement and the weight they carried with the other colonies, Virginia's five resolutions are worth reviewing. They read as follows:

> *Resolved,* that the first adventurers and settlers of this his Majesty's colony and dominion of *Virginia* brought with them, and transmitted to their posterity, and all other his Majesty's subjects since inhabiting in this his Majesty's said colony, all the liberties, privileges, franchises, and immunities, that have at any time been held, enjoyed, and possessed, by the people of *Great Britain.*
> *Resolved,* that by two royal charters, granted by King *James* the First, the colonists aforesaid are declared entitled to all liberties, privileges, and immunities of denizens and natural subjects, to all intents and purposes, as if they had been abiding and born within the realm of *England.*
> *Resolved,* that the taxation of the people by themselves, or by persons chosen by themselves to represent them, who can only know what taxes the people are able to bear, or the

easiest method of raising them, and must themselves be affected by every tax laid on the people, is the only security against a burthensome taxation, and the distinguishing characteristick of *British* freedom, without which the ancient constitution cannot exist.

Resolved, that his Majesty's liege people of this his most ancient and loyal colony have without interruption enjoyed the inestimable right of being governed by such laws, respecting their internal polity and taxation, as are derived from their own consent, with the approbation of their Sovereign, or his substitute; and that the same hath never been forfeited or yielded up, but hath been constantly recognized by the Kings and people of *Great Britain.*

Resolved, that the General Assembly of this colony have the only and sole exclusive right and power to lay taxes and impositions upon the inhabitants of this colony and that every attempt to vest such power in any other person or persons whatsoever other than the General Assembly aforesaid has a manifest tendency to destroy British as well as American freedom.

Opposition to the Stamp Act began to grow as more and more people throughout the American colonies learned how it would affect their everyday lives.

That summer, nine Bostonians (known ironically as the Loyal Nine) met to make plans to oppose the Stamp Act. These men, Boston's first Sons of Liberty, were John Avery Jr. and Thomas Chase, distillers; Thomas Crafts, a painter; John Smith, a brazier; Henry Welles; Stephen Cleverly, a brazier; Henry Bass; Benjamin Edes, a printer; and George Trott, a jeweler. Samuel Adams, also pursuing a vigilant resistance to the act, enlisted such kindred spirits as Dr. Joseph Warren and Paul Revere, a silversmith, in the same cause.

Such groups, formed throughout the colonies, tried to enforce and encourage agreements among the merchants not to import British goods on which an "unconstitutional tax" was levied. Raw materials, formerly sent from America, became scarce in England, causing unemployment there. American orders for British goods declined; consequently, British merchants and manufacturers suffered, so to avoid further losses, they petitioned Parliament to repeal the objectionable Stamp Act.

Colonial merchants, lawyers, printers, and shippers joined in these efforts to have the act repealed, claiming that such taxes served to restrain rather than promote trade. And through their embargo on all trade with Britain, the patriots (as they were called) saw to it that that trade was much reduced. And the men named by the government to distribute the tax stamps were so intimidated by the patriots that they resigned their appointments lest they suffer from mob action.

Despite the tumults it provoked, the Stamp Act did one positive good—even before it went into effect. The colonies, which hitherto had had little communication with one another, now united in protest against the act.

Facsimile autograph of James Otis. His vision of the future America as of November 1768: "Our Fathers were a good people. We have been a free people—and if you will not let us remain so any longer, we shall be a great people."

James Otis of Boston proposed that representatives of the colonies meet in New York City in early October to consult together and to petition the King and Parliament to repeal the offensive act. The resulting Stamp Act Congress, attended by more or less official representatives of the legislatures of nine colonies, was the first representative assembly of the colonies *initiated by themselves* without British authority. Among the 27 delegates were such students of law and government as John Dickinson of Pennsylvania, Henry Ward of Rhode Island, Thomas McKean of Delaware, and Otis himself from Massachusetts. New Hampshire, Virginia, North Carolina, and Georgia were prevented by their governors from sending delegates, but wrote that they would agree to "whatever was done by the congress."

The Stamp Act Congress sent to the King and the House of Commons a declaration of American rights and to the House of Lords a memorial denouncing the Stamp Act and parts of the Sugar Act. An urgent demand for repeal was included that did not fail to mention the damaging effect of these acts on American commerce. The content of the messages was virtually the same as the resolutions of the Virginia burgesses drawn up under Patrick Henry's leadership.

The appeals from manufacturers, merchants, and citizens in Britain as well as America were finally heeded. On March 4, 1766, King George acquiescing, Parliament rescinded the Stamp Act. In a further effort of conciliation, the ministry also reduced the tax on all molasses by two-thirds (to one penny a gallon) and repealed the duty on foreign molasses. The colonists had condemned the Sugar Act as much as the Stamp Act, but Parliament saw fit only to modify, not repeal, the Sugar Act—a mode of concession that would be repeated a few years later with disastrous results.

In order to appease those who disapproved of the concessions to the colonists, Parliament added to the repealer the Declaratory Act, which asserted Parliament's "full power and authority to make laws and statutes of sufficient force and authority to bind the colonies and people of Great Britain, in all cases whatsoever." The Declaratory Act received little publicity, but it did exist; Samuel Adams, for one, never forgot it.

The joyful celebrations held in the colonies on the repeal of the Stamp Act were premature. In 1767 a new chancellor of the exchequer, Charles Townshend, proposed a new measure for raising revenue from the colonies. Parliament then passed the Townshend Acts, named after their author, to become law in America on November 20, 1767. A scheme more offensive to those colonists who held that they had a constitutional right to vote their own taxes would have been hard to devise.

The revenue from this act would be used to pay the salaries of civil officials, maintain an expanded board of customs commissioners, and support troops. The act not only imposed new duties on goods, but provided that general search warrants, known as "writs of assistance," might be used to uncover smuggled goods. Such writs had been vigorously and legally protested as inconsistent with the rights of British subjects by James Otis before the Massachusetts General Court in 1761. Understandably, the Townshend Acts of 1767 revived resistance to the writs and was declared obnoxious in every detail.

By controlling the salaries of civil officials, the ministry would weaken the authority of the local assemblies that had customarily voted those salaries. And the support of a military establishment among them in peacetime had long been a source of irritation to the colonists. To comply with these regulations would be to weld their own shackles.

The items subject to tax under the Townshend Acts were glass, lead, painters' colors, paper, and tea. Yet the colonists, determined to oppose *any* taxation passed without their consent, resolved to do without the taxed items. Tea was to be shunned as if it were poison; home manufactures of all kinds would be encouraged.

One of the most successful steps taken against the Stamp Act was repeated: the association (cooperation) of merchants agreed not to import the articles taxed or indeed any British goods unless or until the taxes were repealed. Prominent citizens and merchants signed the nonimportation agreements, and their names were published in the newspapers so that everyone knew who supported this policy and who did not. Merchants who continued to sell British goods often received rough treatment from their townsmen or were left strictly alone until they saw their error—i.e., that by importing British wares they were supporting Parliament's attempt to "enslave" the colonists, as extremists phrased it.

At last, in May 1770, America heard that the Townshend taxes on all but tea had been rescinded. Bells rang, King and Parliament were again toasted approvingly, and the colonists swore renewed allegiance to them. There remained just one little tax now: the threepence per pound on tea. Small as it was, the tax was very important, for it meant that the British Government held on to its authority and right to impose taxes on the colonies. Also tea was the one item of those taxed from which the greatest revenue could be expected.

Not all members of Parliament supported continuation of the tea tax. On March 5, 1770, for example, former Massachusetts Governor Thomas Pownall argued long and hard against it in the House of Commons. He urged that the tea duty be repealed as superfluous and likely to endanger the relationship between Britain and her American colonies. His motion for repeal failed.

Even Governor-to-be Hutchinson of Massachusetts wrote on October 15, 1770, "I know not what reason may make it necessary to continue the duty on tea; but I think the repeal of it, or making the same duty payable in England, is necessary to prevent disorders in the Colonies."

The smaller the tax, the more dangerous, said John Dickinson in his *Letters from a Farmer in Pennsylvania* that appeared in the colonial newspapers, warning and counseling the colonies. It is easier to fall into the trap and allow a precedent to be set for larger trespasses on the people's liberty, he said.

Another danger was that over the years the colonists had developed a tremendous thirst and taste for tea. Teatime in both England and America had become a favorite social occasion—a time for relaxation and the exchange of news. It has been estimated that at least one-third of the colonists drank tea twice a day. That would, in round numbers, total 500,000 cups a day!

Despite the nonimportation agreements, over 2700 chests of tea were imported by Boston between 1768 (after the Townshend duty became law) and the end of 1772. The publishing of this information in the other colonies did not help Boston's reputation as a stronghold of patriotism.

Even before the nonimportation agreements, colonial traders had found ways of importing tea from Holland or by way of other countries so that they would not have to pay a tax. Tea smuggling was a profitable business in England as well as America. And the colonists enjoyed outwitting the customs collectors, whom they considered merely "placemen"— that is, people holding unnecessary jobs obtained through the influence of a political friend.

But because of this smuggling and because it had overestimated the American market for tea, the British East India Company, one of the largest shippers of tea in the world, found itself with tremendous stocks on hand (17 million pounds). In financial trouble for other reasons too, it had appealed to Parliament for a loan.

Horace Walpole, youngest son of the fabulously wealthy Sir Robert Walpole (a former first lord of the treasury) and a shrewd observer of English affairs, wrote: "The oppressions of India, and even of the English settled there, under the rapine and cruelties of the servants of the [East India] Company [have] created great clamour here."[2] The public suspected that so many great fortunes could not have been honestly acquired. Shareholders and speculators in the company's stock were alarmed when, in September 1772, the company threatened to omit its next half-yearly dividend. This came at a time when London was already in a financial crisis that was spreading to the rest of Europe.

Many members of Parliament who held stock in the company feared that widespread economic depression might follow if it went bankrupt. Some way had to be found to get the company out of its many difficulties.

During 1771 Thomas Hutchinson, the newly appointed governor of Massachusetts and a stockholder in the East India Company, had repeatedly suggested to London that, by lowering the price of the company's tea, the profit from smuggled tea might be reduced so as to make smuggling not worth the risk. Now his suggestion seemed about to be put to the test.

By special act of Parliament, adopted April 27, 1773, the East India Company was authorized to send its tea directly to the colonies, where it could be sold at a much lower price than in England. Who would quibble at a mere three-pence-per-pound tax? That was payable by the consignees (those chosen to receive and sell the tea in America) on arrival. Even with the tax, the tea sent to America would be cheaper than it had ever been before. In this, Parliament believed it had felled several birds with one act: aided the nearly bankrupt East India Company, struck a blow at the tea smugglers, and upheld the British right to tax the colonies. "I am clear," King George III said, "there must always be one tax to keep the right, and as such I approve the Tea Duty."

Many colonists were also clear on this point, but *they* felt that Parliament had *not* the right to tax them since they had no voice in the legislation. Those Americans who clung to their ancient liberties, as they called them, were going to resist. For once the precedent was set and the tax paid, they could expect to be forever taxed—and who knew to what lengths Parliament might go? The colonies might soon find similar taxes and monopolies imposed on other commodities. The moment had come to "keep off whatsoever appears to tend to our ruin or damage," as old Governor Winthrop had said. Yet most of the colonists of English descent revered their home country and sincerely believed that, in time, the king would see that their complaints were just and would take the necessary corrective action. Any other course than petitioning for redress could lead only to disaster.

2. *Bonfire A-Building*

FOLLOWING THE REPEAL of most of the Townshend duties, many colonists were willing to get on with business as usual, but then, in December 1772, another brand was added to the bonfire a-building in Boston. Private letters of Governor Thomas Hutchinson, written to friends in England when he had been the colony's chief justice, and of Lieutenant Governor Andrew Oliver, written when he had been the provincial secretary, were secretly sent to the speaker of the Massachusetts House of Representatives. These ten letters became part of a plan to unseat the governor and his "family" of officeholders. Benjamin Franklin, the sender of the letters, was then the agent in England for Massachusetts and for Pennsylvania; he was also deputy postmaster general for America. Franklin did not say how he had obtained the letters. But, while cautioning that they were on no account to be printed or copied, he did convey a hint that the originals might be *shown* to influential people, even to "some of the Governor's and Lieutenant-Governor's partisans, and spoken of to everybody; for there was no restraint proposed to talking of them, but only to copying."[3]

The letters were in fact read to the Massachusetts House

of Representatives, and a committee was named to report on the meaning of them as it affected the government of the colony. These two high officials (Hutchinson and Oliver), this committee reported, appeared to have been conspiring against the liberties of Massachusetts' citizens. The legislature then sent a petition to the King for the removal of both men from office. The petition, signed by Speaker Thomas Cushing, after accusing these two crown officials of alienating the affections between king and colony, contended that:

> The said Thomas Hutchinson and Andrew Oliver have been among the chief instruments in introducing a fleet and an army into this province, to establish and perpetuate their plans, whereby they have been not only greatly instrumental in disturbing the peace and harmony of the gov't, and causing unnatural and hateful discords and animosities between the several parts of your Majesty's extensive dominions, but are justly chargeable with all that corruption of morals and all that confusion, misery, and bloodshed, which have been the natural effects of posting an army in a populous town.
> Wherefore we most humbly pray that your Majesty would be pleased to remove from their posts in this government the said Thomas Hutchinson, Esquire, and Andrew Oliver, Esquire, who have by their above-mentioned conduct, and otherwise, rendered themselves justly obnoxious to your loving subjects, and entirely lost their confidence: And place such good and faithful men in their stead as your Majesty in your great wisdom shall think fit.

On June 29, 1773, the Massachusetts legislature also sent a complete list of their grievances to Lord Dartmouth, the newly appointed secretary of state for the American department.

After a duel in England between a William Whately and one John Temple, who was accused of having stolen the Hutchinson-Oliver letters, Franklin admitted that he was the one responsible for transmitting them to Boston. A "storm of obloquy" was then directed at Franklin. Whereas he had enjoyed favor and respect from England's ruling class, he now was seen as a radical and a conniving man who would bear watching. Franklin's delay in admitting that he had sent the letters to Boston only added to the appearances against him.

In due time a meeting of the Privy Council would be held to look into the colonists' complaints against Hutchinson and Oliver.

Meanwhile, Parliament had become greatly absorbed in straightening out the affairs of the East India Company. Since this sprawling organization also ruled much of India, many serious problems and effects had to be considered. At last, as a first move toward bringing in some much-needed income to the company, Parliament passed three acts for the better regulation of the company. The first of these, and the only one affecting the American colonies, dealt with the export of the tea that was clogging the company's warehouses.

This act, the East India Tea Act of 1773, which became law on May 10, 1773, set in motion the events that led to what has become known in America as the Boston Tea Party and in England as the Tea Riots. Revoking all other duties *except* the Townshend tax of threepence per pound, the act served to rekindle all the antagonisms of the colonists and to unite both English and American merchants with the colonial radicals. The whole issue would be decided on the spot, and decided forever. The spot was Griffin's Wharf, Boston.

England's watchdogs in the colonies must have been sleeping in the early months of 1773 or they would have noticed the increased activity of the committees of correspondence.

At this time 80 New England towns were in the process of endorsing a circular letter that originated with Boston. The letter opposed the payment of judges' salaries by the Crown out of customs revenues. Among these revenues was, of course, the duty on tea. The colonists feared that if the Crown controlled the salaries of the judges, who were Crown appointees anyway, these men would be wholly independent of and unresponsive to the colonial legislature, which had formerly voted the funds for their salaries.

Leaders in Virginia and Massachusetts had appointed committees of correspondence to exchange views with other colonies on questions of taxation, administration of justice, and other relations with Britain. A "brisk correspondence" among the several colonies was what Samuel Adams said he was happy to see. It meant that the colonists were becoming more aware of their rights and more united in a determination to defend them.

Early in January 1773, Governor Hutchinson added dry wood to the smoldering fire of colonial resentment of Parliamentary acts by his decision to lecture the General Court on Parliament's supreme authority over the colonies, particularly its right to tax. The governor had expressed his opinion privately that "Parliament must give up its claim to a supreme authority over the Colonies, or the Colonies must cease from asserting a supreme legislative among themselves. Until these points are settled, we shall be always liable upon every slight occasion to fresh disorders."[4] Alarmed by the activities of the Boston Committee of Correspondence, he had decided that an outright assertion of Parliament's authority was necessary. But his address failed to impress the General Court. And the House of Representatives did not hesitate to administer a smarting reply, citing legal and historical arguments, prepared by one of the best legal minds in the colony—that of John Adams of Braintree. When this exchange came to the attention of British officials, they termed the governor's action imprudent.

At the same time, Hutchinson was negotiating for the appointment of his sons as consignees of East India Company tea. He was well aware of the plans for shipping the company's excess stocks of tea to America. Yet the full facts about the East India Tea Act did not become public in the colonies until late that summer. In late September, a Philadelphia newspaper printed a letter from London dated August 4 stating that: "The East-India Company have come to a resolution to send six hundred chests of tea to Philadelphia, and the like quantity to New York and Boston; and their intention, I understand, is to have warehouses, and sell by public sale four times a year, as they do here."

Watching the public reaction to this news, a British officer in New York reported: "All America is in a flame. The New-Yorkers, as well as the Bostonians and Philadelphians, it seems, are determined that no tea shall be landed. . . . They have . . . raised a company of artillery, and every day, almost, are practising at a target. Their independent [militia] companies are out, and exercise, every day. The minds of the lower people are inflamed by the examples of some of their principals. They swear that they will burn every ship that comes in; but I believe that our six and twelve pounders, with the Royal Welch Fusiliers, will prevent anything of that kind."[5]

The Sons of Liberty in Philadelphia at once called a meeting of interested citizens. Gathering in the State House on October 18, they declared that the duty on tea was a tax imposed without colonial consent; therefore it was illegal. They adopted the following eight resolutions:

1. That the disposal of their own property is the inherent right of freemen; that there can be no property in that which another can, of right, take from us without our consent; that the claim of parliament to tax America is, in other words, a claim of right to levy contributions on us at pleasure.

2. That the duty, imposed by parliament upon tea landed in America, is a tax on the Americans, or levying contributions on them without their consent.

3. That the express purpose, for which the tax is levied on the Americans, namely, for the support of government, administration of justice, and defence of his majesty's dominions in America, has a direct tendency to render assemblies useless, and to introduce arbitrary government and slavery.

4. That virtuous and steady opposition, to this ministerial plan of governing America, is absolutely necessary to preserve even the shadow of liberty; and is a duty which every freeman in America owes to his country, to himself, and to his posterity.

5. That the resolution, lately entered into by the East India company, to send out their tea to America, subject to the payment of duties on its being landed here, is an open attempt to enforce this ministerial plan, and a violent attack upon the liberties of America.

6. That it is the duty of every American to oppose this attempt.

7. That whoever shall, directly or indirectly, countenance this attempt or, in any wise, aid or abet in unloading, receiving, or vending the tea sent, or to be sent out by the East India company, while it remains subject to the payment of a duty here, is an enemy to his country.

8. That a committee be immediately chosen, to wait on those gentlemen, who, it is reported, are appointed by the

East India company, to receive and sell said tea, and request them, from a regard to their own character, and the peace and good order of the city and province, immediately to resign their appointment.[6]

The citizens then asked the tea consignees in Philadelphia to resign, and they did so. Letters from John Dickinson, the self-styled "Pennsylvania farmer" who was in fact an astute lawyer, alerted the colonies to the ruthless monopoly that was the East India Company. According to Dickinson, "the Laws of Nations, the Rights, Liberties, or Lives of Men" meant nothing to this monolith, which had, "levied War, excited Rebellions, dethroned lawful Princes and sacrificed Millions for the sake of Gain." He called on all Americans to reject the company's plan as dangerous to their liberty. Philadelphians proclaimed the tea plan a plot to enforce the Townshend Duty and anyone aiding it an enemy to his country.

New Yorkers opposed to the tea plan published a news broadside called *Alarm* to meet the crisis. *Alarm* denounced the monopolistic plan and the East India Company, while other newspapers printed threats aimed at the consignees, as well as promises to burn every tea ship that entered New York Harbor. After further demonstrations and uprisings of the citizens, the New York tea consignees at last petitioned the governor to take the incoming tea under the protection of a warship in the harbor. They resigned after some were hanged in effigy or otherwise intimidated.

In Boston the situation was quite different. There the governor's two merchant sons had indeed been designated as agents of the tea. And the governor had been having a running battle for years with the radicals in the town and in the Council, which, he claimed, was now mainly composed of their adherents. He had made clear his determination to uphold the decrees of King and Parliament and was in constant correspondence with the British ministry. It was an unsatisfactory method of communication because of the long delays, but it was the only one available, apart from making a personal visit.

Boston patriots had no trouble in recalling that the Hutchinsons and the firm of Richard Clarke & Sons had been particularly stubborn in selling English tea in earlier years when other merchants had agreed to stand fast against the Townshend tax. With the same two firms appointed to receive the new shipments, Bostonians braced themselves for a contest of wills.

Expecting no opposition to the shipments of cheap tea, the British Government had neither notified the colonial governors of the imminent arrival of the tea ships nor told them what to do in the event of resistance to the East India Tea Act. Without such instructions, the governors were reluctant to take any action in the matter. Hutchinson was in fact hoping that the tea ships would arrive first in New York, where, he knew, Governor William Tryon was "well disposed to do his duty and the people there are less disposed to any violent proceedings as I have reason to think they are here. & an example of peace and good order there may have its influence here."[7]

3. Thomas Hutchinson: Born and Educated Among Us

THOMAS HUTCHINSON served in the government of Massachusetts with honor from 1737 until 1774 and did everything in his power to uphold the law. He said, "I will live and die by the law." However, as his offices and power increased, his popularity declined. Because he was American-born, the people thought he should feel as they did about the acts of Parliament and about representative government. They were the more incensed against him when they found him so implacable in his duty to King and Parliament.

Not only was he American-born, but he represented the sixth generation of his family in America. His most famous forebear was Anne Hutchinson, one of New England's first religious refugees and a woman "of consummate ability and address." After a public trial in 1637, she was expelled from Boston for refusing to compromise her religious beliefs.

The Hutchinson house on Garden Court, Boston. This building was wrecked by a mob in 1765, at the time of the Stamp Act.

Thomas Hutchinson was born on September 9, 1711, in the handsome stone mansion of his father, Colonel Hutchinson, in Garden Court in the North End of Boston. He attended Harvard College, graduating in 1727. Soon afterwards, he became a merchant-apprentice in his father's counting room. His social circle included all the other Boston families who supported His Majesty's Government—the Faneuils, the Bowdoins, the Olivers, and Clarkes. And the woman he married, Margaret Sanford, was the daughter of a governor of Rhode Island.

Hutchinson's political career began in 1737, when he was elected a selectman of Boston and a representative to the General Court, which was the chief law-making body of the province. He later served as speaker of the House of Representatives. One of the major bills he proposed was designed to put the province on a sound financial basis. Though a wise measure, it was not popular. It caused the Land Bank, in which Samuel Adams's father was involved, to fail. Those who lost property and savings when the Bank closed blamed Hutchinson. Yet he had placed the province on a firm monetary basis for the first time in 50 years. Hutchinson was appointed lieutenant governor in 1758, a post he held for 12 years before his promotion to governor.

Although Hutchinson put himself on record as opposed to the Stamp Act, his house was attacked by a mob one late August night in 1765 and he was forced to flee with his family. The crowd, already whetted by rum and probably in search of more, split open the door of his house with axes and proceeded to ransack and destroy his possessions until only the empty shell of the house was left. The approach of daylight stopped them from totally demolishing that.

The lieutenant governor described the scene as one of utter ruin:

> Besides my plate and family pictures, household furniture of every kind, my own, my children's and servants' apparel, they carried off about £900 sterling in money, and emptied the house of everything whatsoever, except a part of the kitchen furniture, not leaving a single book or paper in it, and have scattered or destroyed all the manuscripts and other papers I had been collecting for thirty years together, besides a great number of public papers in my custody. The evening being warm, I had undressed and put on a thin camlet surtout over my waistcoat. The next morning the weather being changed, I had not clothes enough in my possession to defend me from the cold, and was obliged to borrow from my friends. . . . The next evening, I intended [to go] with my children to Milton [where he had a country residence], but meeting two or three small parties of the ruffians, who I suppose had concealed themselves in the country, and my coachman hearing one of them say, There he is! my daugh-

ters were terrified and said they should never be safe, and I was forced to shelter them that night at the Castle.[8] (Castle Island, three miles from town at the entrance to Boston Harbor, was the site of Fort William, where a small contingent of soldiers was stationed.)

Even if the government did compensate him for the loss of his Boston house (valued at about £3000 sterling), Hutchinson said that "a much greater sum would be an insufficient compensation for the constant distress and anxiety of mind I have felt for some time past, and must feel for months to come."

Later he did take his family to his Milton estate, called Unkity Hill, seven miles from Boston. They appeared to enjoy their country home and spent as much time there as possible. Hutchinson sent two of his sons to Harvard College and one to England to be educated. His elder daughter married Dr. Peter Oliver, son of Chief Justice Peter Oliver. The younger daughter stayed with her father and often helped him with his writing of a lengthy work eventually published as *The History of the Colony and Province of Massachusetts Bay*.

Since his instructions came from 3000 miles away, it is not surprising that the governor often felt very much alone and unappreciated. It sometimes took four months for a letter to reach London and for the reply to get back to Boston. It took even longer if debates in Parliament, or discussions with the ministry and the king were necessary.

Meanwhile, like Caesar, Hutchinson was ambitious and his offices and power accumulated, to the dismay of his enemies. He was at the same time lieutenant governor, commander of Fort William, member of the Council, and judge of the probate court. His political opponents felt that one man should not hold so many important posts in the colony; there was a monopoly in government when one family held so much power. Other relatives by blood or marriage held public office, too. His brother-in-law Andrew Oliver was provincial secretary and a member of the Council. When Hutchinson became governor in 1771, Andrew Oliver was made lieutenant governor and his brother, Peter Oliver, was made chief justice of the Superior Court. Foster Hutchinson, a brother, was an associate justice of the Superior Court.

In 1772 the colonists heard an alarming rumor that henceforth the governor's salary would be paid by the Crown and not by vote of the Assembly. When questioned about this, Hutchinson refused to tell the assemblymen whether or not it was true! Communications between himself and the British Government he held to be confidential. But the colonists believed that this matter concerned them too, for if the Crown was to pay his salary, the governor would feel himself less and less answerable to the people.

In 1773 Hutchinson was feeling very "put out," angry, and frustrated. His countrymen no longer troubled to speak civilly to him, he complained, and with all his powers, he could not seem to get anything done. That radical Samuel Adams and his crew were always stirring up unrest. At the moment Hutchinson's private letters were—thanks to the diligent Dr. Franklin and Samuel Adams—being passed around, discussed, and published in the newspapers. And his most straightforward statements and opinions were being twisted against him.

With no one else to turn to, the governor wrote again to Lord Dartmouth in London. He related the troubles he had had over the past seven years with "the first person that openly, in any public assembly, declared for absolute independence." He was referring, of course, to Samuel Adams. Although Hutchinson did not mention Adams's name in this letter, he described Adams's history and character and especially his power over the people. "His chief dependence," wrote the governor, "is upon a Boston town meeting, where he originates his measures, which are followed by the rest of the towns, and of course are adopted or justified by the Assembly." Even when the acts of Parliament to which the colonists objected were repealed, Adams, the leader of the opposition in the Massachusetts' legislature, was not satisfied. He urged his followers to make more demands. As the governor told Dartmouth, "he knows that I have not a Council which in any case would consent to his removal, and nobody can do more than he to prevent my ever having such a Council."[9] The governor saw his own attempts to uphold the laws and the instructions received from England blocked at every turn by that "Master of the puppets," Samuel Adams.

Once the dissension about the tea tax flared up hotly in late November 1773, Hutchinson stayed as much as possible on his Milton estate. Indeed, he deliberated whether or not his regard for His Majesty's service did not *require* him to seek safety at Fort William. He surely was aware that his sons were destined to receive the controversial tea, for he had been corresponding with William Palmer, a London merchant who was prominent in the negotiations with the East India Company and with whom the Hutchinsons dealt with regularly. The governor had written to Palmer in early August: "I wish you may succeed in behalf of my Sons to whom I have given a hint."[10]

Hutchinson and his sons had every reason to do all in their power to insure the safe landing of the teas. Not only were their reputations at stake, but the London merchants who sponsored the consignees had posted in advance a bond or security for the tea shipments. The consignees might be held liable for this if the shipments were destroyed. Even more important, if he should accede to the wishes of the people in opposition to an act of Parliament, the governor would be severely criticized by his superiors in London—and Thomas Hutchinson was anxious to avoid such displeasure.

Upon the governor's actions in the next weeks would depend the success or failure of the East India Company's (some called it Lord North's) plan for winning the New England—and eventually the American—market in tea. Parliament's right to tax the colonies would also be confirmed—or denied.

Thomas Hutchinson's personal seal. It bears his motto: *Libertatem Colo; Licentiam detestor.*

4. *Boston Under Pressure*

Design from the masthead of the *Boston Gazette.* It shows the bird Liberty flying over the town of Boston.

THE *Boston Gazette,* published by Edes & Gill, printers devoted to the liberty cause, gave the radicals' view of the tea plot on October 18, 1773. An editorial in the paper pointed out the dangers of the East India Company scheme, calling it an enticement "to be accessary to our own destruction" and suggesting that the consignees be shipped back to England along with the tea. The act itself was quoted. And in case any reader would be deceived by its legal language, the paper stated that the tea *would* be subject to the Townshend tax.

"Should the Tea now shipping for Boston be returned to England, as it undoubtedly will," the paper said, "if the People do not insist on copying the resolutions of Philadelphia and New York to destroy it; Lord North will meet with a rebuff, which will put his utmost firmness to the Trial. It will be impossible for his Lordship after having exerted all his cunning in flattering the East India company to withstand their peremptory demand of a total repeal of the Tea Act."

In an adjacent column datelined London, the paper ran the following item, in large type:

> Aug. 8. It is reported, that Governor Hutchinson is shortly expected here from America. *God speed him.*

Referring to the British ministry, a columnist remarks:

> "Nothing can be more evident than their aim to get all the trade and property in the empire into their own power—their strides are very large, numerous and hasty; and if they are not vigorously opposed, a community of noble, generous and magnanimous freemen will soon be reduced to a herd of miserable, indigent and spiritless slaves! . . . Perhaps it is not yet too late to free ourselves from popes, devils and locusts. The fifth of November [Guy Fawkes Day] has been for two centuries celebrated in commemoration of such deliverances."

The East India Tea Act was considered an attempt at a monopoly since the East India Company tea, free from export duties by an act of Parliament, would sell at a price below that of smuggled tea even, and the colonial tea dealers who had previously purchased through London agents were eliminated. Moreover, the tea was not ordered by the merchants but was being sent under a license authorized by an act of Parliament.

A circular letter drafted by Samuel Adams and James Warren (of Plymouth) and dispatched to the other committees of correspondence said substantially this: "It is easy to see how aptly this scheme will serve both to destroy the [free] trade of the colonies and increase the revenue [to Britain]. How necessary then it is that each colony should take effectual methods to prevent this measure from having its designed effects."

Expressions of public opinion on the tea scheme began to appear early in November. Americans resented what they saw as a poorly disguised attempt to deceive them—to force, as they said, an illegal tax down their throats along with the tea; to monopolize their trade; and at the same time to use them to bolster a corrupt company for the sake of certain ministerial and other satin-lined pocketbooks.

The Boston consignees received notices from a committee representing the people to appear at Liberty Tree on November 3 at noon to resign their agency in the presence of the citizens. "Fail not at your peril," the notice added. A handbill was also "stuck up at almost every corner" said a Boston merchant. It extended this invitation:

To the freemen of this and neighboring towns:

Gentlemen!

You are desired to meet at the Liberty Tree this day, at 12 o'clock at noon, then and there to hear the persons to whom the Tea shipped by the E. I. Company is consigned, make a public resignation of their office as consignees, upon oath—and also swear that they will re-ship any teas that may be consigned to them by the said Company, by the first vessel sailing for London.

Boston, Nov. 3, 1773   O. C., Sec'y

Show us the men that dare take this down!

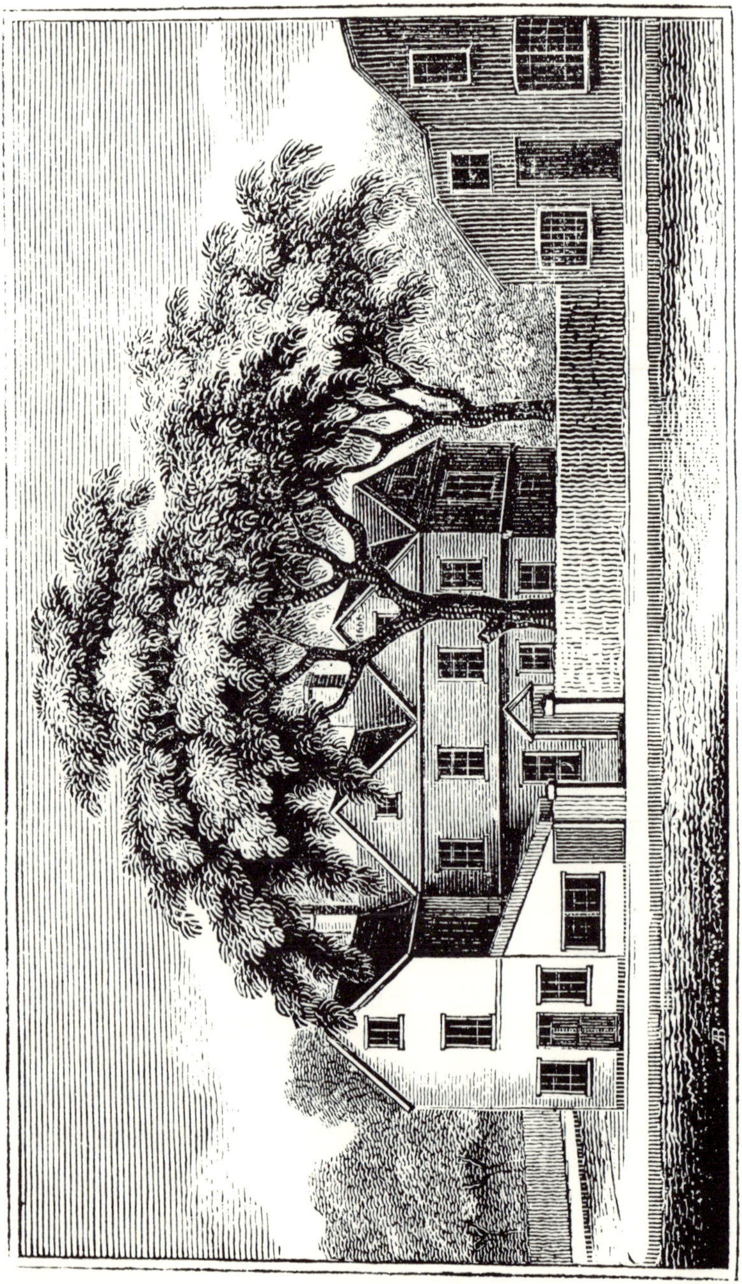

The Liberty Tree at the corner of Essex and Orange Streets, Boston, as it looked in 1774. The tree was cut down by the British during the siege of Boston, 1775-76, at the beginning of the Revolutionary War. Wood engraving from Caleb Snow's *History of Boston*.

Appropriate preparations were made to receive the consignees. A large flag was hung from the Liberty Tree, and church bells rang from 11 to 12 o'clock to summon the people. The consignees did not appear. Governor Hutchinson later wrote an account of what happened next.

> A committee was appointed to acquaint them, at one of their warehouses |where they were holding a meeting of their own] that, as they had neglected to attend, the people thought themselves warranted to consider them as their enemies. |The consignees] treated the message with contempt, and the people, many of whom had followed the committee, forced open the doors of the warehouse, and attempted to enter a room in which the consignees, with some of their friends, were shut up; but meeting with resistance, they soon after dispersed, and the body of the people who remained at the tree, upon the return of their committee, dispersed also. This seems to have been intended only as an intimation to the consignees of what they had to expect. Two days after |November 5], what was called a "legal" meeting of the inhabitants was held in Faneuil Hall. Here the resolves which had been passed by the people of Philadelphia were first adopted; and then a further resolve passed, that the inhabitants of the town, by all means in their power, will prevent the sale of the teas exported by the East India Company, and that they justly expect no merchant will, on any pretence whatever, import any tea liable to the duty. Committees were also appointed to wait on the several persons to whom the teas were consigned, and in the name of the town, to request them from a regard to their characters, and to the peace and good order of the town, immediately to resign their trust.[11]

The consignees all replied that as they had not yet been informed of the terms on which the teas were being sent to them, they could not give a definite answer now. "The answers were all voted to be daringly affrontive to the town, and the meeting was immediately after dissolved," Hutchinson recorded.

The fifth of November (the date on which the Faneuil Hall meeting was held) was Guy Fawkes Day (and night), a reminder of the 1605 Gunpowder Plot and an old English holiday often exploited by political propagandists. In Boston the holiday was celebrated with parades, political symbols and effigies, and often ended in street fighting. The celebration in 1773 must have been as clamorous as usual, for a private letter of that date speaks of "the Noise and disturbance of a turbulant and factious town." The writer, obviously a Crown supporter, goes on:

> The various and discordant Noises with which my Ears are continually assaild in the day, [the] passing of Carts and a constant throng of People, the shouting of an indisciplined Rabble, the ringing of bells and sounding of Horns in the night when it might be expected that an universal silence should reign . . . but instead of that nothing but a confused medley of the ratlings of Carriages, the noises of Pope Drums and the infernal yell of those who are fighting for the possessions of the Devill. . . . I am Led to these thoughts . . . by the very disagreeable situation of this Town in general and some of My Friends in perticular. I have been several days attentively observing the movements of our Son's of Liberty . . . once . . . an honorable distinction. A short Sketch of their procedings may not be [amiss] as nothing in the Papers is to be depended [upon].
> Last Tuesday Morning a considerable Number of Printed papers was pasted up, directed to the freemen of the Province, inviting them to meet at Liberty Tree at 12 oClock the next day to receive the resignation upon Oath of those Gentle'n to whom the [East] India Company have consigned their Tea . . . and their promise of reshiping it by the first opertunity. . . . The next morn'g incendiary Letters were sent at 2 oClock to those gent'n . . . commanding upon their Perril their attendance at 12 oClock at Liberty Tree.

This summons the Gentlemen took no other notice of than by assembling at Mr. Clark's Store, where a considerable Number of their Friends mett them. A little before one o'Clock, a Committee consisting among others of Mr. [William] Molineux, Wm. Denny, [Gabriel] Johonnott, Henderson, Drs. [Joseph] Warren and I think [Benjamin] Church came down (attended by the whole body, consisting of about 300 People) with a Message. . . .[12]

Other efforts were made to obtain the resignations of the tea consignees. For instance, an appeal signed "A Poor Old Man" appeared in the *Boston Gazette* on November 8. From one lone, prophetic voice, it read:

A poor man's wisdom saved a city. I am indeed a friend to Mr. Clarke and his sons, to the two sons of Gv. Hutchinson, and more especially to Mr. Faneuil, whose generous uncle gave us our hall of liberty. And I would earnestly intreat them all to yield without delay to their fellow townsmen.— It may easily be done in a letter to the selectmen.

The three firms concerned were those of Richard Clarke & Sons; Joshua Winslow and Benjamin Faneuil; and the governor's sons, Thomas and Elisha Hutchinson.

Meanwhile, four tea ships were bound for Boston, laden with Bohea and singlo (cheaper kinds of tea), some congo, hyson, and a little souchong. The ships were the *Dartmouth,* commanded by Captain James Hall and owned by Joseph Rotch, a Quaker of Dartmouth, Massachusetts; the *Eleanor,* commanded by Captain James Bruce, John Rowe of Boston; part owner; the *Beaver*, commanded by Captain Hezekiah Coffin, Francis Rotch; part owner; and the *William*, commanded by Captain Joseph Royal Loring and owned by the Clarkes.

Three other tea ships, the *London* bound for Charleston, the *Polly* for Philadelphia, and the *Nancy* for New York, had left England at about the same time. Tensions in these

American cities mounted as the time for the tea ships' landfall drew near. Philadelphians planned to keep them well off from their city, warning Delaware River pilots not to bring them upriver.

Bostonians were under pressure from the other colonies to keep the tea from being landed. If that happened, one writer challenged, "it will confirm many prejudices against them [Bostonians] and injure the common cause essentially in the future." Nearly all of the Boston consignees were known to have been stubborn and late in subscribing to the non-importation agreements of previous years—despite the zealous efforts of Boston's Sons of Liberty. And these same firms were now designated as agents to carry out this new "scheme."

Another town meeting was called in Boston on November 18 to hear the consignees' decision. Again they retorted that it was out of their power to comply with the request of the town because of commercial agreements entered into on their behalf by friends in England. The consignees seemed determined to hold out for a victory for their side.

Governor Hutchinson even tried to enlist the support of his own small military escort. On November 12 he had issued an order to "the Commander of his Excellency's Company of Cadets signifying that . . . it was his wish that they should, one and all, stand ready to be called out for the purpose of aiding the civil magistrates in keeping the peace." The colonel in command of the cadets was John Hancock, a merchant and the moderator of the town meetings then going on (the meetings were termed illegal assemblies by the governor because they were not convened by duly constituted authority). In any case, there is no record of any response from John Hancock to this order.

The Boston consignees were becoming increasingly worried about what would happen when the tea ships—expected momentarily—did arrive. On November 19 the consignees appealed to the governor and Council to take the tea under their protection when it arrived. After some debate the Council postponed a decision. The governor then appointed a committee to review and report on the matter. This report was delayed until November 29, by which date the first of the tea ships, the *Dartmouth,* was inside Boston Harbor. On that date the consignees took refuge on Castle Island. From there they witnessed the arrival of the *Eleanor* on December 2 and the *Beaver* on December 7. Ironically, in addition to the tea that Samuel Adams declared was more to be dreaded than plague and pestilence, the *Beaver* was also carrying smallpox. So the vessel was held off Rainsford Island until she could be cleansed.

The governor was now staying much of the time at Unkity Hill, Milton, far enough from the Boston "mobs." He felt sure that the tea would be landed eventually as it could not be sent out of the harbor without his permission—which he would not give. And if the tea ships should attempt to slip out to sea past the guns of the British warships and of the fort on Castle Island, the tea could not be reshipped to England because of a law prohibiting reimportation. Where could the ships go? To Halifax perhaps, where their controversial cargo might be accepted.

But the governor was not easy in his mind. He had not forgotten the ugly mob of 1765 nor Samuel Adams's boasts of substantial support from the inland towns. Could he, the governor, be responsible for the bloodshed and rioting that would ensue if the warships fired on the town or on the tea ships if they tried to leave? Still without instructions from the British Government on how to handle this matter, he appealed to a friend by letter on November 24, asking for advice "upon the state of the province." *"What am I in duty bound to do?"*[13] he wrote, evidently in great anxiety.

On the other side, those Bostonians who opposed the tea tax knew that they would have to take some action. The patriots in the other colonies recalled that Boston had imported dutied tea before. She might do so again and thus betray the rest of the colonies who opposed the tea tax. Thomas Mifflin, a prominent Philadelphia merchant who had been in Boston that fall when the tea issue began to boil up, put it to the Sons of Liberty: "Will you engage that they [the teas] shall not be landed? If so, I will answer for Philadelphia." And they had pledged their honor.

So both sides braced themselves. The governor could count on cooperation from the customs officials and from Admiral Montagu, in charge of the ships of His Majesty's fleet in the harbor (one of them a 60-gun warship). He could also rely upon the small contingent of loyal troops under Colonel Leslie at Fort William on Castle Island. But it would, he knew, cause great outrage among the people if he were to call upon the military to assist in landing the tea.

As soon as the *Dartmouth* was sighted on November 28, Boston's key patriots were called to important meetings, even though it was a Sunday, a day for rest and worship strictly observed in New England. Yet this proved to be one of the busiest Sundays in the history of Boston to that time.

The selectmen, "having information that Capt. Hall in a Ship from London with Tea on board from the East India Company Consigned Messr. Clarke and others, met at this time in expectation of hearing from Mr. Clark[e]—having waited some time, they then sent to his dwelling House and were informed that he was not in Town—The Board then Adjourned till after Divine Service."

Just the day before, Jonathan Clarke, son of the consignee Richard Clarke, had requested a meeting with the selectmen. They had discussed the whole tea situation with him, telling him that "nothing would satisfy the Inhabitants but reshipping of the Tea to London. . . . After much discoursing . . . he absolutely promised this; that when the Tea arrived nothing underhanded should be done, that the Tea should not be taken out of the Vessel or disposed of in any shape at all; that so soon as the Vessel or Vessels should arrive with the Tea he would immediately hand in proposals to the Selectmen to lay before the Town, that he could not now do it as he did not know what particular Orders he might receive from the Shippers. . . ."

Yet now, on Sunday, Mr. Clarke could not be found. At five o'clock that evening, the selectmen met again. This time, "after waiting sometime in expectation of hearing from Mr. Clark[e], they again sent to his Dwelling house as also to the Houses of some of his Relations, when they were informed that he was out of Town, neither did they know where he was gone; they also sent to the House of Mr. Benjamin Faneuil, another of the Consignees, to inform him that if he had anything to propose to the Selectmen which he would have laid before the Town they were then sitting. The Messenger was told that he was not in Town. The Meeting was then broke up."[14]

The moment the first tea ship arrived, the consignees disappeared!

The Boston Committee of Correspondence also met that Sunday and drafted a letter inviting the local committees of Roxbury, Dorchester, Cambridge, and Charlestown to attend a session at Faneuil Hall at nine o'clock on Monday morning. The printers were busy that Sunday night, for very early the next morning, copies of the following notice were posted up about the town:

> Friends! brethren! countrymen!—That worst of plagues, the detested tea, shipped for this port by the East India Company, is now arrived in this harbour—the hour of destruc-

tion, or manly opposition to the machinations of tyranny stare you in the face. Every friend to his country, to himself, and posterity, is now called upon to meet at Faneuil Hall, at nine o'clock THIS DAY, at which time the bells will ring, to make an united and successful resistance to this last, worst, and most destructive measure of administration.

> BOSTON, November 29.
> Last Saturday arrived Capt. Clark, in a Brig, from London, which he left the latter End of August.—And Yesterday Morning Capt. Hall, in the Ship Dartmouth, came to Anchor near the Castle, in about 8 Weeks from the same Place; on board of whom, it is said, are 114 Chests of the so much detested East India Company's TEA, the expected arrival of which pernicious Article has for some Time past put all these northern Colonies in a very great Ferment:—And this Morning the following Notification was pasted up in all Parts of the Town, viz.
>
> Friends! Brethren! Countrymen!
>
> THAT worst of Plagues the detested TEA shipped for this Port by the East-India Company, is now arrived in this Harbour; the Hour of Destruction or manly Opposition to the Machinations of Tyranny stares you in the Face; every Friend to his Country, to himself and Posterity, is now called upon to meet at FANEUIL-HALL, at NINE o'Clock, *THIS DAY,* (at which Time the Bells will ring) to make a united and successful Resistance to this last, worst and most destructive Measure of Administration.

Column from the *Boston Gazette* of December 20, 1773. This was the report of the arrival of the first tea ship, the *Dartmouth*.

5. *The Ships, the Body Meetings, and the Laws*

THE FIRST of the tea ships to arrive, nine weeks from London, was the *Dartmouth,* carrying 114 chests of tea. She was sighted on Sunday, November 28, when most Bostonians were in church. But alert eyes were on the lookout for these ships. The news that Captain Hall was in port, as the seagoing men of Boston would say, spread quickly. The time for action—and momentous decision—had come.

Governor Hutchinson and the Council met in the council chamber of the Town House that Monday, November 29, to consult "upon means for preserving the peace of the town" and incidentally for breaking up that "unlawful assembly" only a short distance away. A large crowd, which had overflowed Faneuil Hall, was now reassembling at Old South Meeting House "in direct opposition and defiance" of the governor.

The Council now recited to the governor the familiar arguments that the Townshend Acts, of which the tea duty alone remained, was a breach of the colony's charter and that the new tea act was a scheme to undermine the colonists' firm resolve to resist illegal taxation. As to the tea, the councillors did not see that they could assume any responsibility for it.

Meanwhile, the *Boston Gazette* had published some advice regarding the tea consignees' appeal to the Council to take the tea under its protection. For the guidance of the members of the Council, the paper outlined their function: to order and direct the affairs of the province as one branch of the General Assembly. The editorial strongly hinted that if the councillors did give in to the "petitioners'" (consignees') request, they might have to resign. Speaking of (and to) the council members, the paper stated:

> No one it is presumed desires them to resign their appointment; on the contrary as they are too wise a Body to be drawn aside from their Appointment by the Artifices of designing men, it is justly to be expected that they will in this and all other Instances keep precisely to it. The safety of the government and of the people depend much upon it. Their department by no means admits of their condescending to become the Trustees and Storekeepers of certain Factors for the East India Company. As well might they become the Trustees of all the Individuals, and ex officio be the Storekeepers of every Store in the Province; and this it is to be feared would induce such a multiplicity of private Business as to leave them no Time to do the Duties of their Department, viz. the ordering and directing the Affairs of the Province.[15]

In the end, the Council declined to become involved with the tea and advised the governor to take measures for the security of His Majesty's subjects, for the preservation of peace and order, and for preventing all offenses against the law. They then declared the meeting dissolved.

In February 1770 Bostonians had unanimously resolved to abstain wholly from the use of tea. Various substitutes had been tried, and patriotic women had vowed to deny themselves "the drinking of foreign tea, in hopes to frustrate a plan that tends to deprive a whole community of all that is valuable in life"—in short, liberty.

But now, in 1773, it was not a matter of nonimportation agreements. The tea was being sent with the permission and blessing of Parliament itself—and in some instances without the consignees knowing the precise terms under which they were to sell it. Obviously more drastic and immediate measures would have to be taken if the dangerous precedent of paying the tax was to be avoided.

The two parties were at loggerheads, and the laws governing the situation made it more complex. But the patriots were determined to observe the law while showing that they disapproved the taxation.

The laws applying to the tea were as follows:

—A 1724 act of Parliament expressly forbade the reimportation of tea into England. Once exported, the same cargo could not be returned to England; if it was, both the tea and the vessel were liable to seizure by the authorities. This would involve loss to many individuals besides (in this case) the East India Company. This act was well known to Bostonians.

—Under Massachusetts law, incoming shipmasters had to report to the commissioner of impost within 48 hours, and before breaking bulk.

—By another act of Parliament, customs officers could seize goods if the duty on them had not been paid within 20 days after the first entry of the ship at the customs office.

—In order to leave port, a ship had to have a clearance paper from the customs office showing that the applicable duties had been paid.

Bostonians were not seeking to violate these regulations—only to uphold their principles about the tea tax.

That the tea should be returned whence it came "at all events" was the unanimous decision of some 5000 citizens, including many from nearby towns, who assembled in Old South Meeting House on Monday, November 29. It was an extraordinary meeting, not the usual town meeting convened by order of the selectmen (although some of them were present). It was only the first of several such mass meetings. The people attending were sometimes referred to as the Body, or this Body, and their sessions became known as the Body meetings.

In the afternoon session that Monday the citizens became more specific in their demands, calling upon Francis Rotch, who represented the *Dartmouth's* owner, not to "enter" that vessel's cargo at the customhouse until the next day, Tuesday, November 30. They also ordered a watch of 25 men to be set on the ship, now lying at Griffin's Wharf.

The Body made repeated efforts on Monday and Tuesday to get a reply from the consignees as to what they were prepared to do. When none came, Francis Rotch and Captain Hall were asked to pledge to return the tea to London on the same ship in which it had arrived. Under pressure, the two men reluctantly agreed, although Rotch declared that he would protest the proceedings.

Meanwhile, on Monday the governor ordered the justices of the peace to be alert for any disturbances in the town and "to suppress any riots that may happen". It was the sense of the meeting of the Body that this action did not reflect honor on the people and was "solely calculated to serve the views of Administration."

On Tuesday morning a disappointing letter from the consignees was read to the assembled people. It merely stated that the consignees could do nothing to satisfy the people's request, but offered to have the tea stored until they could get further instructions from the company.

On this same Tuesday morning the sheriff read to the people a message from the governor stating that their meeting was in violation of the law and calling on them to disperse. The message was rejected with a hiss by the assembled citizens.

According to the law, severe punishments could be applied if 30 or more persons persisted in unlawful assembly after such a proclamation was read; and if they were armed, the Riot Act could be invoked. Obviously, in this case, the governor did not have sufficient forces on hand to back up such an action. And any such action would only have aggravated an already serious situation. Hutchinson was later criticized for failing to take more aggressive action.

Boston was put on a state of military alert from November 29 on. The watch over the tea ships was maintained day and night, John Hancock and Samuel Adams taking their turns along with other patriots. Sentries were set in church belfries and church bells were to be rung in case of danger. Tar barrels were kept ready on Beacon Hill to be lit to signal the country towns, and six post riders were ready to gallop out on call.

In meeting after meeting, the pressure of public opinion was exerted on the consignees (absent though they were), the ship owners, and the captains to get them to return the tea "whence it had come." Representing his father, the owner of the first ship to arrive, Francis Rotch received the brunt of attention.

Only 23 years old, Rotch was a Nautucket-born Quaker. He belonged to the second generation of a family of merchants that had long engaged in the whaling and mercantile trade with both industry and integrity. The young man reflected credit on himself throughout the troublesome business of the tea. Naturally he was anxious to save the *Dartmouth* and its cargo from destruction by overzealous patriots or from seizure by the customs authorities, either of which could happen.

On Thursday, December 2, Rotch was permitted to unload the *Dartmouth* of all goods except the tea. The ship's log noted, "Began to deliver our goods, and continued to land them from day to day, till Saturday, December 11, having a guard of 25 men every night."

On December 7 Rotch went out to Castle Island to talk to the consignees and ask them to take the tea off his hands. They refused, although earlier in the year when the tea plan had been devised some of them had exerted themselves to get the consignments.

On December 8 Governor Hutchinson instructed Admiral Montagu to block all channels out of the harbor with his warships.

By December 15, three of the four tea ships—the *Dartmouth, Beaver,* and *Eleanor*—were tied up at Griffin's Wharf.[16] Holding the main supply of goods for the winter trade, they had to be brought up to the wharf for unloading.

According to law, the duty on the *Dartmouth*'s tea would have to be paid by December 17, when the 20-day limit was up.

Meanwhile, on Tuesday, December 14, Rotch was again sent for by the Body in Old South Meeting House and asked whether he was prepared to comply with the wishes of the people regarding the tea on board his father's vessel. At this point Rotch retorted that his earlier promise to comply had been made out of fear and without legal advice. Since then he had consulted lawyers and now realized that to give in to the demands of the people would mean his ruin. He would go as far as any man for the good of his country, but he "could not see the justice of his being put in the Front of the battle." After all, no one had offered to bear the loss of the vessel or to share the loss if that should happen.

Rotch was then ordered to apply immediately to the customhouse collector for a clearance, and a committee was appointed to accompany him to the collector's office. Then the Body adjourned until Thursday, December 16.

The collector, Richard Harrison, knew well the Bostonians' dislike of customs duties. He postponed giving a reply until he had consulted with the comptroller. Harrison said he would give an answer at ten o'clock the next morning, Wednesday. According to the committee's report, Mr. Rotch called upon these two officials the next day and made the demand in the following manner:

> "I am required and compelled at my peril by a Body of people assembled at the Old South Meeting-house yesterday ... to make a demand of you to give me a clearance for the ship *Dartmouth* for London, in the situation she is now in, with the tea on board."

Upon which one of the Committee observed that they were present by order of the Body only as witnesses of the before-mentioned demand, and the answer that should be given.

Thereupon Mr. Harrison, the Collector, said to Mr. Rotch (Mr. Hallowell, the Comptroller, being present), "Then it is you make this demand?" Mr. Rotch answered, "Yes, I am compelled at my peril to." Then Mr. Harrison said to Mr. Rotch, "Your ship, *Dartmouth,* entered with me the 30th November last, with dutiable articles on board, for which the duties have not been paid. I cannot therefore give you a clearance until she is discharged of those articles, consistent with my duty."

Report of these transactions was made to the meeting of the people the next day.

6. Boston Harbor a Teapot

THURSDAY, December 16, dawned a dull, dark day. A cold rain was falling. Its icy drops fell on the tea ships still lying at Griffin's Wharf and on the people doggedly making their way once more to Old South Meeting House. This would settle it, surely, they thought—the duty deadline for the *Dartmouth* was at hand.

There had been much conferring and discussion, both public and private, the day before. Now, at ten o'clock on this Thursday morning, the Body heard the report of the committee that had accompanied Rotch to see the customs officers. Rotch himself was sent for again. When he appeared, a motion was made that "this Body expect that he immediately protest against the Custom-house, and procure a pass of the Governor, and that he this day proceed with the vessel for London."

Rotch replied that such an order was impracticable. When he was again asked whether he would order the *Dartmouth* to sail that day, he said he would not. Therefore, "Mr. Rotch was desired to proceed in making protest and demanding a pass" for the ship.

On such a day cautious citizens stayed at home. The tea

consignees and their friends were already living on Castle Island, protected by the troops under Colonel Leslie. The warships *Active* and *Kingfisher* were guarding the channels out to sea, and Admiral Montagu had orders to permit no unauthorized vessels to pass. The patriots were "in a web of inextricable difficulties," Governor Hutchinson now believed. Boston's selectmen had been working night and day to resolve the deadlock between the consignees and the people, but "all our efforts" said one of them, "could not produce an agreement."

Rotch had not only consulted the best lawyers in Boston, but had taken almost every conceivable step to free the *Dartmouth*. So far, his efforts to get a pass for the ship and at the same time to satisfy the demands of the people had been fruitless. The only step left was to appeal to the governor, the highest authority in the colony. Rotch was instructed by the Body to do so.

Meanwhile the meeting would be adjourned until 3 P.M. to give Rotch time to ride the seven miles to Milton, consult with the governor, and return to Boston.

Rotch had a fairly lengthy conference with Hutchinson who had long ago prepared his stand. The two men did discuss another course of action: the governor offered to give Rotch a letter to Admiral Montagu asking the admiral to furnish the *Dartmouth* all necessary protection. In other words, the *Dartmouth* would be towed out to take refuge under the guns of the fleet. Once there, no doubt, the tea could be removed and stored on Castle Island until the temper of the people had cooled. Rotch concluded that it would be a difficult and dangerous maneuver and that he would incur the people's anger, for they would interpret this as treachery on his part. He declined the tempting letter. He could see nothing but disaster if he accepted it. Then the governor refused to give the pass as it was his duty to uphold the Acts of Trade. Rotch was forced to return to the meeting with this negative reply. The appeal to the governor had accomplished nothing.

Meanwhile, the opponents of the tea tax were preparing to act, for few believed that the governor would back down on the issue. While Rotch was with Hutchinson, certain Boston gentlemen met in the parlor of Benjamin's Edes's house. Peter Edes, the printer's young son, was stationed in another room, making punch for them. "They remained in the house till dark," he recalled, "I suppose to disguise themselves like Indians, when they proceeded to the wharves where the vessels lay."[17] Some of the party used the Long Room over Edes's printing office to put on their disguises; others used the Green Dragon Tavern.

On the dark afternoon of December 16, 1773, certain other picked men—mechanics, apprentices, and even a group from Maine—found that blankets, hatchets, paint, lamp-black and chimney soot were needed in the work they had to do.

Darkness had set in by the time Rotch rode into Boston, long past the time set for his return. It was about a quarter to six, and after a long, lonely trip in the cold rain, he had to face the impatient crowd still jamming the meetinghouse. Worst of all, he could offer no solution to the problem.

Over the past three hours the meeting of the people had been harangued by a variety of orators. Now the brilliant young lawyer, Josiah Quincy Jr. was addressing them. As Rotch approached the entrance, he could hear Quincy's melodious, powerful voice, as the lawyer warned:

> The exertions of this day will call forth events which will make a very different spirit necessary for our salvation.

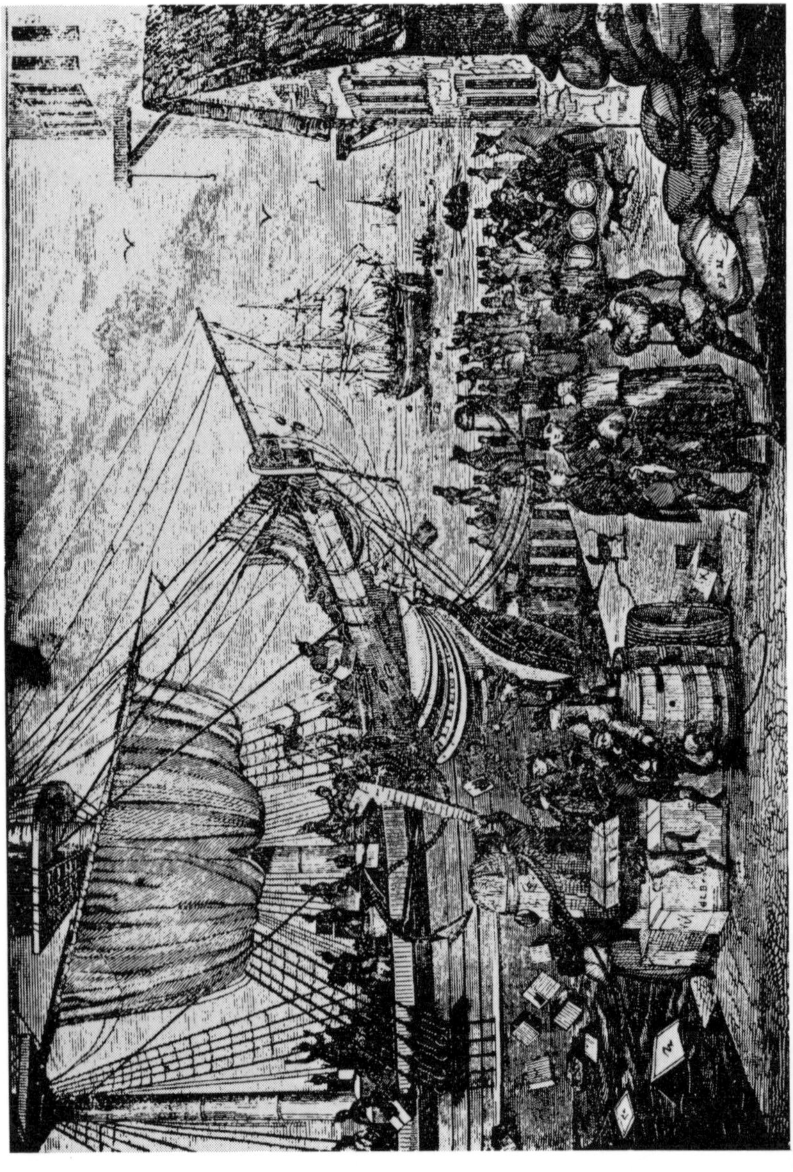

Destruction of the tea in Boston Harbor, December 16, 1773. Engraving by Robert P. Mallory, from a painting by George L. Brown.

Look to the end.... We must be grossly ignorant of the importance and value of the prize for which we contend; we must be equally ignorant of the powers of those who have combined against us; we must be blind to that malice, inveteracy, and insatiable revenge which actuates our enemies ... to hope we shall end this controversy without the sharpest, the sharpest conflicts. Let us look to the end. Let us weigh and consider before we advance to those measures which must bring on the most trying and terrible struggle this country ever saw.[18]

Resolutions had already been taken by the citizens that they "should not suffer the landing of the tea." When Rotch came in and gave his negative report from the governor's own lips, hotheads shouted "A mob! A mob!" But the moderator, Dr. Thomas Young, quickly restored order. Pointing out Rotch's valiant efforts to cooperate with them, Young pleaded that the merchant should not suffer any harm to his person or property. Then Rotch was asked whether he would send his vessel back to London with the tea. He replied that to do so would be his ruin. Would he land the tea then? He replied that "he had no business with it unless he was properly called upon to do it, when he should attempt a compliance for his own security."

At this point, Samuel Adams concluded, "This meeting can do nothing more to save* the country." Then suddenly appeared the red-and-black painted faces of Indian warriors near the door. Shouts rang out and were answered from inside the meetinghouse: "Boston harbor a teapot tonight!" and "The Mohawks! The Mohawks have come!" Gleeful cries filled the hall, and some of the audience left at this break. But the meeting was again called to order, and Samuel Adams moved that Dr. Young, the moderator, be asked to address the

---

*Rotch reported this word as "serve."

people. Young then spoke for 15 or 20 minutes on the unhealthy effects of tea on the constitution. He hoped his countrymen would hereafter abstain from all use of it and also stand by each other should any be called to an account for their proceedings. "He affected to be very merry and when he had done, the audience paid him the usual tribute of applause . . . and immediately [the moderator] dissolved the meeting."[19]

Meanwhile, others had had a headstart in making for the tea ships. Those who had stayed in the meetinghouse for the last speech now crushed to the doors. They saw people muffled up in various disguises heading for the wharves. They plunged down Milk Street toward Griffin's Wharf, gathering stragglers and fresh Indian braves on the way.

The crowd followed and watched the Mohawks take charge of the three tea ships with no opposition. The night was now clear and the moon shining. The hatchets were put to work and the holds of the ships *Dartmouth, Beaver,* and *Eleanor* were laid open. The tea chests were hoisted on deck, cut to pieces, and the tea—£9,000 worth—was poured overboard. The Mohawks worked with precision, in three teams, accomplishing their task with a minimum of noise and confusion while thousands of onlookers watched approvingly. By ten o'clock the deed was done.

7. *Aftermath*

THE first general feeling in Boston after the destruction of the tea was one of relief—even on the part of the governor, who had worried about the effect of his final refusal to Rotch. "He was relieved from his suspense, the same evening, by intelligence from town of the total destruction of the tea," Hutchinson recalled in his *History of Massachusetts Bay.*

He realized then, if not before, that the only way the tea could have been landed was by force—yet, he thought, neither the marines on the warships nor the small regiment at Castle Island would have been strong enough to "have kept possession of the town." Had Admiral Montagu ordered his warships to fire on the town, it would have meant the destruction of innocent people and created even greater public outrage.

John Rowe, one of the merchants involved, had had misgivings about the tea from the beginning. He was part owner of the *Eleanor,* which had arrived on December 2 with 80 whole chests and 34 half-chests of tea.

A threatening letter, signed only "Determined," had been delivered to Rowe on November 28. This had agitated the 58-year-old man so much that he had not gone to church that day. He had been called before the Body and questioned

Boston 17 Dec.' 1773

Sir,

I wrote to you the 8.'th instant and informed their Lordships of the rebellious state of the People of this Town on account of the Teas exported by the East India Comp.'y subject to the Kings Duty of three pence in the pound; which was resolved in the Town Meeting should not be paid, and on that account an armed Force was appointed to parade the Wharfs where the Tea Ships lay to prevent its being Landed.

I am now to desire you will be pleased to inform their Lordships that last Evens between 6 & 7 o'Clock, a large Mob assembled with Axes &c.ª encouraged by M.' John Hancock, Sam.'l Adams, and others and marched in a body to the Wharfs where the Tea Ships lay, and there destroyed the whole by starting it into the Sea.

I must also desire you will be pleased to inform their Lordships that during the whole of this transaction neither the Gov.' Magistrates, Owners, or the Revenue Officers of this place, ever called for my Assistance if they had I could easily have prevented the Execution of

this

Philip Stephens Esq.'

this plan, but must have endangered the Lives of many innocent People by firing upon the Town.

I am,
Sir
Your most Obedt
humble Servt
J Montagu

Reproduction of a letter from Admiral Montagu, reporting the destruction of the tea on December 16, 1773. Courtesy of British Museum, London.

on several occasions, and he had asked the citizens whether a little salt water would not do the tea good, or whether salt water would not make as good tea as fresh. This the people applauded.

Feeling unwell, Rowe remained at home all day and all evening on Thursday, December 16, and again the next day—even though a new ship he had ordered was being launched at Walker's yard. "The affair of Destroying the Tea makes Great Noise in the Town," he noted in his diary on December 18. "Tis a Disastrous Affair & some People are much Alarmed. I can truly say, I know nothing of the Matter nor who were concerned in it. I would rather have lost five hundred Guineas than Bruce [Captain of the *Eleanor*] should have taken any of this Tea on board his Ship."[20]

Eyewitnesses confirmed that Samuel Adams, John Hancock, Dr. Joseph Warren, Dr. Thomas Young, Josiah Quincy Jr., William Phillips, Mr. Cooper, William Molineux, Mr. Scollay Jr. (a Boston selectman), John Pitts (also a Boston selectman), Dr. Church, Mr. Greenleaf (late a justice of the peace), and Thomas Cushing were in almost constant attendance, and the first eight were the chief speakers at the tea meetings.

"What every body supposed impossible after so many men of property had made part of the meetings and were in danger of being liable for the value of it . . . [had happened]," wrote Hutchinson to former governor Francis Bernard, in London. But Hutchinson was unrepentant for his part: "It would have given me a much *more* painful reflection if I had saved . . . [my reputation] by any concession to a lawless & highly criminal assembly of men, to whose proceedings the loss must be consequently attributed, & the probability is that it was a part of their plan from the beginning."[21]

John Adams, the thoughtful young lawyer from Braintree who was known for his careful defense of the British soldiers accused of the so-called Boston Massacre of 1770, had spent long nights and years in the study of law. Yet he concluded that the destruction of the tea was "the grandest event which has ever yet happened since the controversy with Britain opened. The sublimity of it charms me!" But, he admitted, "The die is cast. The people have passed the river and cut away the bridge."[22]

To his diary he confided more: "This however is but an Attack upon Property. Another similar Exertion of popular Power, may produce the destruction of Lives. . . . What Measures will the Ministry take, in Consequence of this?—Will they resent it? will they dare to resent it? Will they punish us? How? By quartering Troops upon us?—by annulling our Charter?—by laying on more duties? By restraining our Trade? By Sacrifice of Individuals, or how."[23]

To his friend James Warren, in Plymouth, he wrote that "Suits and prosecutions, Armies and navies . . . military executions, charters annulled, treason trials in England, and all that . . . are all but imaginations. Yet, if they should become realities, they had better be suffered than the great principle of parliamentary taxation be given up."

"Yesterday [December 21]," Adams wrote to Warren, "the Governor called a council at Cambridge. Eight members met at [Brigadier] Brattle's. . . . The Governor, who last Friday was fully persuaded and told the council that some late proceedings [the destruction of the tea] were high treason, and promised them the attendance of the attorney-general to prove it them out of law books, now, such is his alacrity in sinking, was rather of opinion they were burglary. I suppose he meant what we call New England burglary, that is, breaking open a shop or ship, &c., which is punished with branding. . . ."

Early on the morning of December 17, Hutchinson had driven to Boston to meet with the Council, but no business could be done since a quorum was not present. He spent that night at Castle Island, visiting his sons and no doubt conferring with the other consignees and officials there. At last, he met with the Council on the following Tuesday in nearby Cambridge. The councillors were "much divided in their opinion" and not inclined to take any action, he reported. The attorney general, Jonathan Sewall, was ordered to lay the case of the destruction of the tea before the grand jury, who, Hutchinson wrote later, could not be expected to "ever find a bill for what they did not consider as an offence."

The destruction of the tea, Hutchinson felt, was "the boldest stroke which had yet been struck in America."[24] He knew that this attack on private property would anger the British Government and he recognized that his own authority was at the vanishing point. There were few leaders to whom he could turn for support, at least on this side of the Atlantic.

The news of Boston's tea party traveled fast. The Boston patriots had immediately sent express riders to announce the action to the committees of correspondence in New York and Philadelphia. Would the other colonies stand by Boston and give her at least moral support? When their bold action brought approval and promises of economic aid, Boston patriots were excited—and enormously relieved.

On December 28 Samuel Adams wrote that "The ministry could not have devised a more effectual measure to unite the colonies." He had sent a long report to Arthur Lee, the colony's agent in London, referring him to the bearer, Mr. Hugh Williamson of Philadelphia, for particular details. Williamson had attended the Body meetings in Boston and reported that they were pervaded with as much dignity and sobriety "as [in] the British Senate." (See eyewitness report in

Appendix II of this book.) Meanwhile, Samuel Adams was pressing on with plans for a Continental Congress.

The tea landed in Charleston, South Carolina, was allowed to remain in storage there until it rotted while the tea ships arriving off New York and Philadelphia were not permitted to land, or even come near the wharves, but returned to England with the tea untouched.

In New York, in December, even some tea brought in the *London* for a private customer was thrown overboard, and "had the company's ship come to the wharf she would probably have been burnt."

At a meeting of the Dealers in Teas in Boston, held on Thursday evening, December 23, 1773, at the Royal Exchange Tavern, King Street, it was voted to sell the tea stocks on hand until January 20, 1774, but not thereafter. "From that time we will suspend the Sale of all Teas, until the Sense and determination of the Inhabitants of the Seaports, and other Towns in the province can be known, with respect to its total or partial expulsion." In addition, the dealers voted that "We will not at any time hereafter purchase on our own account, or receive on Commissions, or otherwise, any Teas whatever," and that "We will not ourselves make use of Tea, nor will we permit it in our respective Familys from and after the time limited for selling, but will do our utmost to discourage it in others. . . ."

This meeting of about 43 men was composed of both Tories, or "loyal" members, and Whigs, or patriots.

A town meeting of Charlestown, Massachusetts, held on December 28 voted not to "buy, sell or suffer to be used in our families [any India tea] till the British Act of Parliament imposing a duty on the same shall be repealed." The people took every ounce of tea on hand to the public market square where it was burnt at high noon—"an example well

T E A,
DESTROYED BY INDIANS.

YE GLORIOUS SONS OF FREEDOM, brave and bold,
    That has stood forth----fair LIBERTY to hold ;
Though you were INDIANS, come from distant shores,
Like MEN you acted-----not like savage Moors.
CHORUS.
    Bostonian's SONS keep up your Courage good,
      Or Dye, like Martyrs, in fair Free-born Blood.
Our LIBERTY, and LIFE is now invaded,
And FREEDOM's brightest Charms are darkly shaded :
But, we will STAND---and think it noble mirth,
To DART the man that dare oppress the Earth.
    Bostonian's SONS keep up your Courage good,
      Or Dye, like Martyrs, in fair Free-born Blood.
How grand the Scene !----(No Tyrant shall oppose)
The T E A is sunk in spite of all our foes.
A NOBLE SIGHT---to see th' accursed TEA
Mingled with MUD----and ever for to be ;
For KING and PRINCE shall know that we are FREE.
    Bostonian's SONS keep up your Courage good,
      Or Dye, like Martyrs, in fair Free-born Blood.
Must we be still--- and live on Blood-bought Ground,
And not oppose the Tyrants cursed sound ?
We Scorn the thought----our views are well refin'd
We Scorn those slavish shackles of the Mind,
" We've Souls that were not made to be confin'd."
    Bostonian's SONS keep up your Courage good,
      Or Dye, like Martyrs, in fair Free-born Blood.
Could our Fore-fathers rise from their cold Graves,
And view their Land, with all their Children SLAVES ;
What would they say ! how would their Spirits rend,
And, Thunder-strucken, to their Graves descend.
    Bostonian's SONS keep up your Courage good,
      Or Dye, like Martyrs, in fair Free-born Blood.
Let us with hearts of steel now stand the task,
Throw off all darksome ways, nor wear a Mask.
Oh ! may our noble Zeal support our frame,
And brand all Tyrants with eternal SHAME.
    Bostonian's SONS keep up your Courage good,
      And sink all Tyrants in their GUILTY BLOOD.

TEA Destroyed by Indians. A broadside issued in 1774. From the collection of the Library of Congress.

worthy of imitation," commented the *Boston Gazette*. Other towns followed suit. The strength of feeling in the country towns of Massachusetts was expressed by their appointing a committee "to inspect Tea Drinkers, and if they shall know or find out any Person who shall still continue to Use, Sell, or Consume in their families any East India Tea, to post up their name in some public place, that they may be known and Despised."

Ripples from Boston's tea party fanned out into other towns, where anyone found to have any quantity of tea became suspect. On January 7, 1774, the town of Colerain, Massachusetts, informed the Boston Committee of Correspondence that "Bohea Tea is very plenty at Northampton received in a clandestine manner as is suspected . . . it is reported that the Bohea Tea that was cast ashore at the island of Nantucket is transported up Connecticut River." Replying on March 1, the Boston Committee said, "It must come from some other quarter than you have suspected, 54 chests and a third out of 58 cast on shore being now locked up in a store at the Castle. The others were sold to some miscreants at the Cape, but are since destroyed by the Indians in that neighborhood." "Indians" everywhere regarded tea as a dangerous, un-American herb.

In March 1774 John Adams was still speculating on what might happen. On the morning of March 7 he had read the "News . . . from England of a Duel between Mr. Temple and Mr. Whately, and Mr. Franklins explicit Declaration, that he alone sent the Governors Letters to Boston . . . and great Things are to be laid before Parliament &c. &c. Twenty Eight Chests of Tea arrived Yesterday, which are to make an Infusion in Water, at 7 o'clock this evening."[25] He had this last bit of news *in advance*!

Boston then held her *second* tea party on March 7, 1774 —the tea sent on the ship *Fortune*. This clearly demonstrated that the patriots were determined never to swallow dutied tea and that they had no regrets about the first act of defiance. The news of this second tea party truly shocked the members of Parliament when they heard of it in May and defeated any tendency to be lenient toward Boston.

The tea sent to Boston had disappeared, and the consignees were carefully keeping out of sight during this time of tension. Nevertheless, this handbill was distributed about town:

> Brethren, and Fellow Citizens!
> You may depend that those odious miscreants and detestable tools to Ministry and Government, the Tea Consignees (those traitors to their country, butchers, who have done, and are doing, every thing to murder and destroy all that shall stand in the way of their private interest) *are determined to come* [from Castle Island] *and reside again in the Town of Boston!* I therefore give you this early notice, that you may hold yourselves in readiness, on the shortest warning, to give them such a reception as such vile ingrates deserve.
>   Joyce, Jr.
>   (Chairman of the Committee for Tarring
>   and Feathering)
> If any person should be so hardy as to tear this down, they may expect my severest resentment.

The Hutchinsons were attempting to return to a normal life but it was still risky. One son, Thomas Jr., stole back to his father's house in Milton in early January for a few days after six cold weeks of living on Castle Island. He had to return to the island, but before leaving, Thomas wrote to his brother Elisha:

Mr. Faneuil and myself coming off, caused a suspicion that we intended for Boston, which was the means of Saturday's notification, which I sent you. Mr. Faneuil is since returned to the Castle; and I am really more confined than if I was there, as I keep pretty close to my room. Mr. Jonathan Clarke sails in a few days for England ... of which I am very glad, as it may prevent misinterpertation of our conduct on that side the water.[26]

Thomas also mentioned an incident involving Elisha, who had married Polly Watson of Plymouth in June 1772. When Elisha and Polly went to visit her parents there on January 17, 1774, bells of the town were tolled (the signal in time of danger), causing a crowd to gather in front of the Watson house demanding that the couple leave town. Because of the late hour and severe weather, Polly's father asked that they be allowed to stay overnight. But when they did not leave early enough the next morning, the crowd drove them out into a great snowstorm." They found a refuge with Chief Justice Peter Oliver and his family in Middleborough.

Elisha and the chief justice visited Plymouth on January 27. The Watson house was now guarded by friends armed with guns and hot water, but "a tribe of Indians ... bootcap'd Mr. Hutchinson's sleigh." On Sunday, Elisha went to meeting (church). However, Colonel Watson (Polly's father) had to promise the townspeople that Elisha would leave as soon as the sleigh was repaired; he left that afternoon. Clearly the animosity of the people toward the governor's family and the tea consignees was unabated.

Thomas Hutchinson Jr. wrote to his brother, "I am sorry it [the Plymouth incident] hapned, as it will be a harvest for Edes & Gill, but it can't be helped. . . . I intend to employ somebody to collect what debts I can, but suppose we are generally considered as outlawed."

Writing to Elisha on February 4, Thomas said their father "seems determined to go to England, unless prevented by the Lt. Governor's declining state, which I think increases upon him very fast. What do you think of giving up the Store? I am told it is kept shut up & the few things in it may easily be removed."[27]

Evidently the Hutchinsons were coming to the conclusion that their days in the colony were numbered, and that they would be happier in England—at least until the flames of rebellion had subsided.

The governor had been uneasy in his post for some time, especially since the publication of his private letters in the public press the previous June. He was well aware that the colonists had petitioned for his removal. To Lord Dartmouth he had written in July 1773, "I humbly hope I shall be honorably acquitted and that I shall not be left wholly without employment and support in advanced life, for my private fortune is not sufficient unless I sink below the moderate living I had always been used to before I came to the Chair. I have my youngest son in England entirely unprovided for."[28]

On August 7, 1773, however, he had written to England that "The flame which was raised with so much art by means of the private letters of the Governor and Lt. Governor and the Resolves [connected with them] . . . appears to me to have much subsided for several weeks past. The most sensible people . . . when they came to read the letters being convinced that they gave no grounds for the Resolves and prejudices. . . ."

To Lord Dartmouth he wrote:

> I desire to submit to the great Governor of the World who orders all events in perfect righteousness. It is grievous to be vilified and reproached by so great a part of the people, but the histories of all countries and all ages show that the

Vulgar or common people are easily led away by artful designing men. Some of the best men of all orders assure me they are my friends and *principibus placuisse viris** affords me no small comfort. I am notwithstanding almost tired of my public character and whensoever it shall be the pleasure of the king to *relieve* me I shall consider it as really a *relief* from a burden which is greater than they who do not feel it generally imagine. In the meantime let me ask your prayers that I may be faithful & let me ask them also for my Country. I have it from very good authority that *the effectual fervent prayer of a righteous man availeth much.*†[29] [Emphasis is Hutchinson's throughout.]

---

*Part of a quotation from the Latin poet Horace. It can be translated briefly: "To have pleased the great is no slight honor."
†New Testament, James 5:16.

8. *How the News Was Received in London*

GOVERNOR HUTCHINSON'S report on the destruction of the tea went to London on the brig *Dolphin,* Captain James Scott commanding. It arrived at Gravesend (a port near London) on January 27, 1774—a fairly fast transatlantic sail for that kind of ship and for a winter passage. But another ship had already arrived from Boston carrying eyewitnesses of the Boston Tea Party. The *Hayley,* owned by John Hancock, put in at Dover on January 19 and reached Gravesend on January 21. The news of the tea's destruction was rushed by express rider from Dover to London, together with copies of the Boston newspapers, even before the ship docked at Gravesend. By the evening of January 19 the King knew of the tea party, and so did the chairman of the East India Company.

Soon Lord Dartmouth was asking to have a conversation with the captain of the *Hayley.* On January 25 the ship *Polly* docked at Gravesend with the tea rejected by Philadelphia. And soon afterwards Lord Dartmouth interviewed the East India Company's agent from that port. Dartmouth was compiling a dossier on all the tea business. It would eventually be placed before Parliament for consideration.

Such shocking news could not have come at a worse time for Benjamin Franklin and the rebellious colonists. Many officials and members of Parliament were still out of town after the Christmas holiday. The affairs of the East India Company had occupied them during the preceding session of Parliament to the exclusion of almost any other issue, so they felt entitled to a rest from their labors. Yet now the same venomous problem was raising its head again.

The chairman of the East India Company had heard in late December that Boston would resist the landing of the teas; he in turn had advised Lord Dartmouth. Now the company was faced not only with the resistance but with a loss of £9,659—and possibly much more.

On December 25 a London newspaper had published Benjamin Franklin's admission that he was responsible for having sent the Hutchinson-Oliver letters to Massachusetts. That colony's petition for the removal of their governor and lieutenant governor was to be heard by The Committee of the Privy Council for Plantation Affairs on January 11, 1774. The hearing was postponed to January 29 after Franklin, acting as colonial agent for the Massachusetts House of Representatives, had asked for a delay and been granted it. By the time definite word about the destruction of the tea in Boston had reached England, controversy about America was at the boiling point.

Franklin was in hot water and he knew it. A suit in chancery was also being brought against him because of the purloined letters. Now he found that Governor Hutchinson was to be represented before the Privy Council by Alexander Wedderburn, England's solicitor general no less, who "reserved the right" to inquire just how the letters were obtained.

Franklin quickly employed two lawyers of his own, knowing that among other things he faced the possible loss of his office as deputy postmaster general for America. When the news of the tea's destruction came, he took pains to characterize it as "an act of violent injustice." He also stated that he thought Boston should be required to pay compensation to the East India Company for the loss of the tea.

At the Privy Council meeting on January 29, Wedderburn launched a scathing attack on Franklin that was not only without precedent, but scarcely relevant to the matter before them. His ironic thrusts at the Massachusetts agent were enjoyed to the full by the largest attendance of the council in some time. Only Lord North and Franklin remained unsmiling during Wedderburn's attack. Franklin, wearing a new dress suit of Manchester velvet, stood "conspicuously erect," reported one of the audience, "without the smallest movement. . . . The muscles of his face had been previously composed so as to afford a placid tranquil expression and he did not suffer the slightest alteration of it to appear during the speech in which he was so harshly and improperly treated."[30]

Shortly after this meeting, Franklin was notified of his dismissal from his post office position, and he knew himself to be in deep disgrace. The charges against Governor Hutchinson and Lieutenant Governor Oliver, on the other hand, were dismissed as having been "founded upon . . . false and erroneous allegations; and calculated only for the seditious purposes of keeping up a spirit of clamour and discontent in the said province."

In a way, Franklin was caught on his own hook if he *had* sent the letters to America with mischievous intent. The incident had not helped the Massachusetts patriots' cause, but had instead stiffened the British Government's resolve to administer stern punishment.

On the evening of January 29—only a few hours after the Privy Council meeting—seven cabinet ministers met to discuss the colonial situation. They agreed "that in consequence of the present disorders in America, effectual steps to be taken to secure the Dependence of the Colonies on the Mother Country." In the minds of the British ministers, the Boston Tea Party had raised the fundamental question of sovereignty.

General Thomas Gage, then in London, wrote to Governor Hutchinson on February 2 that "The fate of the Teas at Boston and Philadelphia is known, but no account yet from New York. People talk more seriously than ever about America: that the crisis is come, when the Provinces must be either British Colonies, or independent States. What will be done, nobody I believe can yet tell. People talk, and I apprehend publish their own, or the conjectures they have heard from others. Nothing can be fixed. . . ."[31]

Gage himself would have considerable influence on the turn events would take. As a professional soldier with about 18 years' experience in the American wilderness as well as at Montreal and New York, Gage was now invited to a private audience with King George, who asked him to give his views on the American situation. Before returning to England on leave in the summer of 1773, Gage had been commander in chief of the British military forces in America.

In his conference with the King, Gage remarked that "They [the colonies] will be Lions, whilst we are Lambs, but if we take the resolute part they will undoubtedly prove very meek." This made a profound impression on the King, probably because it agreed with his own way of thinking. After this talk, King George asked Lord North, his first lord of the Treasury, to hear Gage's ideas on how to compel "Boston to submit to whatever may be thought necessary." Since Gage also said that the rebels could be crushed with little added expense of troops, he was soon on his way back to America as military governor of Massachusetts Bay Colony, replacing Governor Hutchinson who had already been given a leave of absence.

At about the same time—on February 2, 1774—Horace Walpole commented prophetically: "We have no news public or private; but there is an ostrich-egg laid in America, where the Bostonians have canted three hundred chests of tea into the ocean, for they will not drink tea with our Parliament. ... I believe England will be conquered some day or other in New England or Bengal. . . . and we may be undone a twelvemonth before we hear a word of the matter—which is not convenient, and a little drawback on being masters of dominions a thousand times bigger than ourselves."[32]

9. *Lord North*

THE FIRST LORD of the Treasury of Great Britain at this time was by background and character not one to appreciate the symbolism of such an act as the destruction of the tea at Boston. He saw it as defiance of an act of Parliament that he was sworn to uphold and as the destruction of private property that he was sworn to protect. It was, to North's mind, the act of a crowd of hooligans, of which he saw all too many in London itself.

Frederick North was educated at Eton College and at Trinity College, Oxford. At the age of 20, he had taken the traditional Grand Tour of Europe with his half brother (the future Lord Dartmouth). North married Anne Speke of Dillington, Somersetshire, in 1756. It was a good marriage, better than most at that time for they were a happy, well-matched pair, if not handsome.

His first post in government service was a junior lordship in the Treasury Department. Though not a brilliant speaker, North *became* a good debater; also, he was devoted to his duty and served his government with some distinction over a period of 12 years in Parliament.

He became chancellor of the exchequer after the death

of Charles Townshend, author of the Townshend Acts, and, three years later, in 1770, first lord of the Treasury. For the next 12 years, North was in charge of the finances of his country, a post of heavy responsibility.

Lord North. From a caricature by Boyne. Reproduced with permission of The Longman Group Ltd., from W. Baring Pemberton, *Lord North* (London: Longmans Green & Co., Ltd., 1938).

George III, who was more than five years younger than North, came to the throne in 1760 and soon found that he could rely upon the ductile North to support and execute his ideas. Since 1754 the borough of Banbury had returned North to the House of Commons as a member. By the time of the East India Company business, North had established himself in the mind of the King and in the opinion of his peers as one who could be depended upon to carry out his duties with devoted adherence to British tradition.

Those acquainted with Lord North spoke of his "notorious irresolution," but once his attention was fixed on his purpose and duty, he adhered to it with all the tenacity of a dog with a bone between his teeth. His ability to "sleep" through the long harangues that members of Parliament endured resulted in some enjoyable moments. On one occasion, when a well-known drone was scheduled to speak, North had left instructions to be awakened when, if ever, the speaker reached contemporary times in his discussion. The instructions were obeyed, but North, aroused and hearing a reference to the reign of William III, turned to his neighbor and convulsed the house by exclaiming clearly, "Zounds, sir, you have woken me up a century too soon!"

Several rural retreats were necessary to provide escape from the heavy burdens of his office. When Parliament was in recess and gentlemen went to their country estates or to Bath, North could generally have his choice of Bushey Park, near Twickenham, not far from London; Dillington in Somerset; or Waldershare, near Dover, in Kent. The King made him Ranger of Bushey in 1771.

A constant prey to feelings of inadequacy, North frequently came to the point of surrendering his seals of office, only to be persuaded to stay on by his friends and the King, who leaned heavily upon his first minister. The following description is probably a fair one: "He presided personally over the Commons, then very much the senior partner in the body politic. There, the glance of his bolting eyes kept watch and ward over his friends and supporters. His wit entertained them. His dexterity kept them up to the mark. His conciliatory manner humored them. His comfortable, solid form, whether upon its feet, turning a laugh against an opponent, or slumbering away unconcernedly while adversaries prophesied the eclipse of their country, created a feeling of confidence."[33]

North could more easily understand and sympathize with a Hutchinson than with an Adams of Massachusetts Bay. He had himself been the target of an "ugly-looking London mob" during the troubles fomented by John Wilkes. As North was approaching the House of Commons one day, the crowd closed in on his carriage and smashed it to matchwood, and a bully pushed a staff into his face. Luckily another minister arrived on the scene in time to rescue him. Much cut and shaken up, the abused Lord North nevertheless marched into the house and "astonished the assembly by making a firm and unhurried speech."

Frederick North remained first lord until 1782 and was ill at ease most of the time, or so he said. Gibbon, the historian, knew North well and wrote of him in 1778 that while "the two greatest countries in Europe are fairly running a race for the favour of America, I fear our *Lord* has more bottom than foot."

Sir Winston Churchill, a much later prime minister and also a historian, summed up Lord North: "A charming man, of good abilities and faultless temper, he presided over the loss of the American colonies." Sir Winston cited as "a fatal blunder" the act of Parliament authorizing the East India Company's monopoly on tea.

10. *Riots and Proceedings*

THE AMERICAN COLONISTS, at least some of them, were convinced that there was a conspiracy to systematically deprive them of their liberties and to keep them in subjection to Great Britain—hence the use by colonial writers of "slavery," "corruption," "Egyptian taskmasters," "designing men," and other terms that seem harsh and exaggerated to us. Patriot leaders such as Samuel Adams, Arthur Lee and even the conservative John Dickinson used a kind of verbal violence to arouse and awaken the people's dormant sense of their rights and to make them realize that these rights would be eroded unless the process was resisted and reversed. The word "subdue" occurred so often in the British Government's references to the colonies that there can be no doubt of the government's intention in the 1770s.

British letters and documents of the time refer to the destruction of the tea at Boston as a "riot" or "riots" or as "proceedings" in a way that suggests the "proceedings" were anything but orderly or legal; Governor Hutchinson's phrase was "unwarrantable proceedings." For years, the ministry, informed by Massachusetts governors Bernard and Hutchinson and the Olivers, had been conditioned to believe that *all* gatherings of the Boston populace were riots. Sons of Liberty in New York, Philadelphia, and Charleston were at least as forceful in their determined efforts to refuse the tea, and they protested sooner than those in Boston. But the tea ships arrived first at Boston, which was therefore put to the test first, and the Boston consignees proved to be more unyielding and evasive than those in the other cities.

That violence *might* be used was implied in the notices sent to the tea consignees who were roused in the middle of the night or at dawn to receive messages ordering them to resign their appointments. For example, a "committee" of several hundred citizens went to the Clarkes' store on November 3 to interview them after they failed to resign at Liberty Tree and to tell them that they were therefore considered enemies of the people. Some of this group became irritated and stormed the door, but no one was injured. On November 17 a small crowd pounded on the door of the Clarkes' house on School Street. One Clarke son threatened to fire on them unless they went away. When he did fire, the people smashed the windows, frames and all, and threw stones in. Some of the occupants were grazed, it was said, and some furniture was damaged.

Although the leaders in the town were keeping a close rein on the unruly, the consignees felt threatened and moved out to the fort on Castle Island as soon as the tea ships began to arrive. The governor spent much of this time on his country estate in Milton.

There was rioting in the streets of London and other English cities during this period, so it is little wonder that "riot" became a term indiscriminately used in the press and in private and public statements. Any public gathering that showed signs of becoming raucous or threatening was termed a "mob." Nevertheless, American and English "mobs" of this period aimed at specific, limited targets—at the repeal of an "obnoxious" act or tax rather than the complete overthrow of the government. "Mob" disturbances, therefore, were bloodless actions for the most part.

Sons of Liberty in Boston took pains to show that the tea meetings were orderly—illegal perhaps, according to government views, but orderly. And in those meetings, as Governor Hutchinson himself noted, "many men of property, besides the selectmen and the town clerk" were active.

Immediately after the destruction of the tea on December 16, the Boston Committee of Correspondence sent the following notice to the other colonies:

> Gentlemen,
>   We beg to inform you in great haste that every chest of tea on board the three ships in this town was destroyed the last evening *without the least injury to the vessels or any other property* (author's emphasis). Our enemies must acknowledge that these people have acted upon pure and upright principle."

Mercy Otis Warren, in her history of the Revolutionary War, for which she was able to obtain firsthand accounts, reported that after the dissolution of the Body Meetings "there appeared a great number of persons, clad like the aborigines of the wilderness, with tomahawks in their hands and clubs on their shoulders, who without the least molestation marched through the streets with silent solemnity, and amidst innumerable spectators, proceeded to the wharves, etc. . . . This done, the procession returned through the town in the same order and solemnity as observed in the outset. . . . No other disorder took place, and it was observed the stillest night ensued that Boston had enjoyed for many months. . . ."[34]

Yet Governor Hutchinson, reporting to Lord Dartmouth on December 17, used the word "violence." He said, "What influence this violence and outrage may have I cannot determine; probably [the Council] may issue a proclamation promising a reward for discovering the persons concerned, which has been the usual proceeding in other instances of high-handed riots." Having been the victim of a mob that demolished his house in 1765, Hutchinson was hardly an impartial observer. And it must be evident to the reader that contemporary accounts of these events were, more often than not, highly charged with personal feeling and political bias.

11. *Measures Against Boston*

ON FEBRUARY 4, 1774, definite decisions were taken in London in response to Boston's act of protest of December 16, 1773. First, Lord Dartmouth proposed to the cabinet that the seat of government in Massachusetts be moved from Boston and that the customs officers also be removed to "such other port as shall be judged most convenient." Second, the cabinet agreed to consult the attorney general and the solicitor general as to whether or not the "riots" in Boston amounted to the crime of high treason, and, if so, who could be charged with the crime and "what will be the proper and legal method of proceeding against such persons."

The Crown's lawyers reported to the cabinet on February 11 that the acts and proceedings in Boston did amount to high treason and named individuals who could be charged with the crime. Among those mentioned as possibly chargeable were Messrs. Molyneux, Denny, Warren (presumably Dr. Joseph), Church, Adams (presumably Samuel), Young, Williams, "the moderator of the Assembly [Body meeting] ... and the several persons, called a committee of correspondence, who readily accepted that commission, and acted in appointing the armed watch, and Hancock, one of the same watch. . . ."

But, the lawyers pointed out, the activities of these men would have to be established in evidence—in a trial. Would the Crown be able to produce witnesses who would testify against the alleged offenders? There were grave doubts on this score. Nevertheless, Lord Dartmouth—perhaps urged by the King—pressed the matter. Twelve people who had recently arrived from Boston were interviewed about the events that had taken place there in November and December. Their sworn statements were then examined by the Crown lawyers, who notified the cabinet on February 28 that "the charge of High Treason cannot be maintained against any individuals on the ground of the depositions taken . . . on the 19th inst."

Assured of the legality of withdrawing customs officers from Boston—tantamount to closing down the port—Lord Dartmouth and other government officials now proceeded with these actions. Certain ministers felt strongly that the executive branch of Massachusetts government needed strengthening. The Massachusetts Council was the object of special concern since Colonel Leslie had reported that it had refused to permit his troops to enter the town to suppress the tea "riots." But in order to change the government (or constitution) of a colony, the ministry had to place the whole matter before Parliament. This raised the vital question—precipitated by the defiant destruction of the tea—of the dependence or independence of the colonies.

King George's message relating to the "outrageous Proceedings at Boston" was presented by Lord North to Parliament on March 7, 1774. The King laid the whole matter before his two Houses of Parliament so that they could "take steps to put an immediate stop to the present disorders," and consider "what further regulations and permanent provisions may need to be established for better securing the execution of the laws and the just dependance of the colonies upon the crown and parliament of Great Britain."

In placing the Boston Port Bill before Parliament on March 14—the first of a series of bills to subdue Boston and the Massachusetts Bay Colony—Lord North observed that the destruction of the tea marked the third time that officers of customs had been prevented from doing their duty in Boston Harbor; he thought the inhabitants of the town deserved punishment. "It was no new thing for a whole town to be fined for such neglect," he said. "Boston had been upwards of seven years in riot and confusion and associations had been held against receiving British merchandise so long ago . . . that Boston had been the ringleader in all riots, and had at all times shewn a desire of seeing the laws of Great Britain attempted in vain. . . . That the act of the mob in destroying the tea, and other proceedings belong to the act of the public meeting, . . . other colonies were peaceably and well inclined towards the trade of this country, and the tea would have been landed at New York without any opposition, yet, when the news came from Boston, that the tea was destroyed, Governor Tryon [of New York], from the advice of the people, thought that . . . it would be more prudent to send the tea back to England than to risk the landing of it. . . . Boston alone was to blame for having set this example, therefore, Boston ought to be the principal object of our attention for punishment."

North also proposed a clause in the bill that, he said, would prevent the Crown from restoring Boston's privileges until full compensation had been made to the East India Company for the loss of its tea. Other clauses, "of more nice disquisition," would be proposed later.

He added that "at Boston we were considered as two independent states; but we were no longer to dispute between legislation or taxation, we were now to consider only whether or not we have any authority there; that it is very clear we have none, if we suffer the property of our subjects to be destroyed." He hoped that all—both peers, members, and merchants—would agree with him, about proceeding unanimously to punish such parts of America as denied the authority of Britain. "We must," he said, "punish, control, or yield to them."[35]

Only two members of the House of Commons protested the fairness of the foregoing and said they would oppose the port bill.

North insisted, in answer to arguments, that "we must proceed with firmness and without fear or they [the colonies] will never reform; if we exert ourselves now with firmness and intrepidity, it is the more likely they will submit to our authority."

For many months, as Lord North's March 14 speech shows, the British Government thought that it had only to subdue Boston and Massachusetts Bay. Also, it was inclined to listen only to those whose opinions confirmed its own. For years, Governor Hutchinson and the governors before him had been almost the only heeded source of information about the colony. And these governors, as we have seen, held their own biased views of the Bostonians and emphasized their troubles with the radicals in Massachusetts, particularly Boston. As a result, there was, as one 20th-century historian has commented, "utter lack of comprehension of each side with regard to the other."

Assuming the role of parent, the government thought it obvious that when "the children" were disobedient and destructive punishment should follow.

The punitive acts against Massachusetts passed by Parliament as a result of the Boston Tea Party were called in America the Intolerable Acts. They were:

—The Boston Port Bill, an act closing the port of Boston to commerce from June 1, 1774, until the King by proclamation or order of council, should see fit to open it. The act also provided for moving Massachusetts' seat of government from Boston to Salem and its customs office from Boston to Plymouth. Boston would be restored to its former status only when it paid for the tea destroyed and signified its submission to the authority of Parliament. Precisely how this submissive attitude should be shown was not made clear.

—The Massachusetts Government Act, under which the colony's Council would be Crown-appointed rather than, as formerly, elected by the House of Representatives with the governor's approval; judges, sheriffs and other law enforcement officers would be appointed by the governor; and town meetings, except for the yearly one necessary for the election of town officers, could be held only with the governor's consent.

—The Impartial Administration of Justice Act, which permitted the governor to remove trials to another colony or even to England if he felt this was necessary to insure a fair trial for anyone indicted for carrying out acts of Parliament or for anyone indicted for a crime "committed while engaged in suppressing riots or enforcing the revenue laws."

This new system of government for Massachusetts centralized power in Crown-appointed officials and reduced popular participation to a minimum. While these three acts were designed for Massachusetts, the other colonies could readily read the threat to themselves.

A fourth act passed by Parliament on May 9, 1774, amended the 1765 Quartering and Mutiny Act to permit troops to be billeted in occupied private houses if necessary. Although this amendment applied to all the troops in North America, it was designed to prevent a situation like that of December 16, 1773, when Colonel Leslie's regiment had been barracked on an island three miles from the place where a show of British military strength might have been useful.

The Intolerable Acts made it possible, too, for the Massachusetts governor to call on the military for assistance in putting down disorders, *without having to get the consent of the Council*. He could also issue pardons where "necessary to the due administration of justice" in case of a disorder such as the so-called Boston Massacre of 1770.

One of the colonists' most persistent complaints had been of the quartering of troops among them in peacetime. The new regulations were bound to revive the old resentment. And the choice of a military man as the new governor further emphasized the punitive nature of the acts and the at least implied threat of force. General Thomas Gage was not to be envied his new assignment.

12. *Will Boston Submit?*

ON APRIL 9, 1774, John Adams was still gloating that "the tories were never, since I was born, in such a state of humiliation as at this moment." But, he added, "News we have none. Still! silent as midnight! The first vessels may bring us tidings which will erect the crests of the tories again, and depress the spirits of the whigs."[36] For his own part, Adams did not think war would come at this time.

On May 10, after months of anxious waiting, the people of Boston received news of passage of the port bill on arrival of the ship *Harmony,* five weeks out of London. "The severest act ever penned against the town," was the considered opinion of the merchant and tea consignee John Rowe.

As Bostonians realized the seriousness of the blow to their trade, events began to move with unaccustomed speed. On Friday, May 13, Samuel Adams moderated a town meeting at Faneuil Hall called to discuss the port bill. After an opening prayer, the bill was read and the inhabitants invited to consider "what Measures are proper to be taken upon the present Exigency of our public Affairs, more especially relative to the late *Edict* of a British Parliament for Blocking up the Harbor of Boston, & annihilating the Trade of this Town." A committee was appointed to report their sense of what steps should be taken. Also, the Boston Committee of Correspondence was "desired to dispatch Messengers with all possible speed to the other colonies and the several towns in this Province" to acquaint them with the state of affairs. The letter intended to convey this news to the other towns and colonies was read and approved in an afternoon meeting. It called for unity and mutual support in resisting these oppressive acts and pointed out that Boston was suffering in the common cause.

Also it was voted that, if the other colonies would agree to stop all importations from and "exportations to Great Britain & every part of the West Indies, till the Act for Blocking up this Harbor be repealed, the same will prove the Salvation of North America & her Liberties: On the other Hand, if they continue their Exports & Imports, there is high Reason to fear that Fraud, Power & the most Odious Oppression, will rise triumphant over Right, Justice, Social Happiness & Freedom—And moreover, that this Vote be forthwith transmitted by the Moderator to all our Sister Colonies in the Name & behalf of this Town."

While this meeting was in session, the new military governor of Massachusetts Bay, Thomas Gage, arrived in Boston Harbor on His Majesty's ship *Lively*. He was ready to test his vigorous-sounding recipe for subduing the Americans: "If we take the resolute part they undoubtedly will prove very meek." Gage had instructions to use his troops to preserve order if necessary. He was also to collect evidence against the ringleaders of the tea party, the punishment of whom the King considered "very necessary and essential."

The "perfect crisis"* was at hand, for without support from other colonies Boston could not exist and her long-sustained efforts to "resist tyranny" would fail. Her need brought forth Samuel Adams's and Joseph Warren's most eloquent appeals for help. Paul Revere, Boston's most trusted confidential courier and Son of Liberty, was sent off to New York and Philadelphia with the circular letter, which said in part:

"The people receive the edict with indignation. It is expected by their enemies, and feared by some of their friends, that this town singly will not be able to support the cause under so severe a trial. As the very being of every colony, considered as a free people, depends upon the event, a thought so dishonorable to our brethren cannot be entertained as that this town will be left to struggle alone."

The other colonies were asked to join in suspending all trade with the "Island of Great Britain" until the act blocking up Boston's port "be repealed."

Revere also distributed to other towns along his way copies of the baleful act, edged in black and headed with a skull and crossbones surmounted by a crown.

On the evening of his arrival in Philadelphia, patriots there met to consider the Boston letter and concluded that the time had come to hold a general congress of all the colonies. The idea was not new, for Samuel Adams had started a move for this as early as September 27, 1773, when he wrote in the *Boston Gazette*: "As I have long contemplated the subject with fixed attention, I beg leave to offer a proposal to my fellow-countrymen, namely, that a CONGRESS

---

*Dr. Thomas Young, the moderator of the Body meeting on December 16, 1773, wrote to a friend in New York: "The perfect crisis of American politics seems arrived and a very few months must decide whether we and our posterity shall be slaves or freemen." (As quoted in *The Boston Tea Party* by Benjamin Woods Labaree.)

OF AMERICAN STATES be assembled as soon as possible; draw up a Bill of Rights, and publish it to the world; choose an ambassador to reside at the British Court to act for the United Colonies; appoint where the Congress shall annually meet, and how it may be summoned upon any extraordinary occasion." Citizens of Boston had been reminded of the desirability of such a congress by a March 1774 lecture that John Hancock delivered in commemoration of the Boston Massacre.

Immediately after receiving Boston's call for support, groups of citizens in other colonies gathered to discuss the situation. After all, as Samuel Adams often remarked, "the colonies are all embarked in the same bottom [vessel]." Eighty-nine delegates of the then-dissolved Virginia House of Burgesses met at the Raleigh Tavern in Williamsburg on May 27 and agreed to boycott all East India Company goods, especially tea. They further agreed that a congress of all the colonies was urgently needed to discuss the crisis. The resolutions taken at this meeting were sent to the other colonial assemblies, and many of them approved the idea of a congress.

Shocked by the harshness of the Intolerable Acts, colonists who previously could not decide which side was right now moved to join the radicals. Conservative Philadelphians, however, went so far as to suggest that Boston might consider paying for the tea destroyed. Yet when the port bill took effect on June 1, Philadelphia—like many other colonial cities and towns—publicly demonstrated its sympathy for Boston. On that day all business halted, church bells tolled as for a funeral, and flags were kept at half-staff.

While most of the colonies agreed to sustain Boston with shipments of food and economic aid, they would not agree to the stern economic boycott on Britain that Boston had called for—at least, not until more conciliatory action had been tried. The proposed general congress was therefore necessary to get an agreement among the various colonies as to what their next move should be.

Even the moderate Boston merchant, John Andrews, was forced to agree with those who held that a tyrranical government was in power. In his diary he wrote:

> We must acknowledge and ask forgiveness for all past offenses, whether we have been guilty of any or no; give up the point so long contested; and acknowledge the right of Parliament to d..n us whenever they please; and to add to all this, we must pay for an article unjustly forced upon us with a sole view to pick our pockets (not that I would by any means justify the destruction of that article). When that is done, where are we? Why, in much the same situation as before, without one flattering hope of relief; entirely dependent on the will of an arbitrary Minister who'd sacrifice the Kingdom to gratify a cursed revenge. A more convincing proof we can't have than in the present Act for blocking up our Port, which could not have been more severely and strongly express'd if all the Devils in the infernal regions had had a hand in the draughting it.[37]

In February 1774 Benjamin Franklin had written to the leading Massachusetts patriots (Thomas Cushing, Samuel Adams, John Hancock, and William Phillips) to advise them that: "As the [East] India Company . . . are not our Adversaries, and the offensive Measure of sending their Teas did not take its Rise with them, but was an Expedient of the Ministry to serve them and yet avoid a Repeal of the old Act, I . . . hope that before any compulsive Measures are thought of here, our General Court will have shewn a Disposition to repair the Damage and make Compensation to the Company. . . . A speedy Reparation will immediately set us right in the Opinion of all Europe. . . ."[38]

Samuel Adams appears to have pigeonholed this letter, but on May 18 George Erving, a Boston merchant, offered to contribute £2,000 toward payment for the tea destroyed.

When this offer was made known to the town meeting it "was in general rejected." In a final decision on the matter, on June 17, the Boston town meeting decided not to pay for the tea because such action would constitute an endorsement of the port bill. In so voting, the colonists took another step along the road to independence.

General Gage had arrived in Boston Harbor only a little after Governor Hutchinson received from Lord Dartmouth the news that he was being replaced. Dartmouth had written: "General Gage's continuance in the Government will most probably not be of long duration."

Hutchinson was now free to follow his previously expressed desire to go to England to consult with the ministers in person. There was the usual elegant entertainment for the incoming governor in Faneuil Hall and a farewell address to Hutchinson signed by many distinguished Boston Tories. A separate address was also written and presented to Hutchinson by the selectmen and principal inhabitants of Milton. Their complimentary words must have given some comfort to the old gentleman (he was nearly 63) as he faced a new chapter in his life. He sailed for England on June 1, 1774, with his son Elisha and daughter Peggy. He believed he would be reinstated as governor of Massachusetts Bay whenever Gage's services were no longer required there.

On the ship, he could hear church bells tolling for the loss of Boston's port privileges and see her citizens dressed in mourning for the same reason. Could he appreciate their attitude in any way or was he congratulating himself on his dedication to his duty? As the ship moved out into the Atlantic perhaps he was writing another page in his *History of the Colony . . . of Massachusetts Bay.*

13. *Condemned Without a Hearing*

WHAT CONCILIATORY MOVE by the British might have saved the situation? If a cabinet minister or a commission had been sent to America to talk to "the other side"—to listen to the colonists' grievances—with an open mind, could Britain have still retained her American colonies? Even now it is hard to choose a person who might have succeeded in this. Ex-governor Hutchinson would obviously not have been a good choice. As for Franklin, the psychological wounds he had sustained at the Privy Council meeting had been allowed to harden into scars of bitterness against Britain.

Edmund Burke,* raising his voice in Parliament on behalf of America in April 1774, had cried out angrily, "We are more likely to drive them to arms by refusing to hear them than by any other means." Yet the powerful men on the government side—the King, Lord North and his friends—had seemed set on a collision course with the colonists ever since

---

*Then agent for the lower house of the New York Assembly and a member of the House of Commons. Considered a friend of America, Burke had made a powerful plea in the House of Commons for repeal of the tea tax.

the repeated rejections of the tea had made their meaning felt in Britain.

Even those British merchants who had something to lose in cutting off the American trade were unaware of the seriousness of the situation until too late. On March 18, before Parliament had passed the port bill, the merchants who traded with the Northern colonies had offered compensation to the East India Company for *double* the value of the tea destroyed —but the offer was discouraged by Lord North himself. He advised them to return to their counting houses and leave everything to him—a further sign that the king was determined to subdue the rebellious colony.

Threepenny piece of reign of George III. Courtesy of the British Museum.

Of the agents representing the colonies in London, the only two that were on the scene at the time when they might have at least protested the government's policy were Arthur Lee and William Bollan. Franklin was still in England, but he was in public disgrace. A belated secret effort to involve him in a conciliation move was not begun until the end of November 1774, and it failed just prior to his departure for America in March 1775. Nevertheless, Franklin's messages to leaders in America during the year he remained in England after the Tea Party seemed to sustain rather than quench a spirit of independence.

Arthur Lee, agent in London for the Massachusetts House of Representatives, was hardly in a better position than

Franklin. The British Government knew that Lee approved of the committees of correspondence in America. Earlier, Governor Hutchinson had acquired copies of Lee's advice to Massachusetts and sent them to Lord Dartmouth, labelling them "highly criminal" and "mischievous." On March 18, 1774, Arthur Lee wrote to his brother, Richard Henry Lee,* from London in reference to the Boston Port Bill:

"If the colonies in general permit this to pass unnoticed, a precedent will be established for humbling them by degrees, until all opposition to arbitrary power is subdued." He cautioned, however, that their reaction should be "well weighed" and that any "manifestos" should be "prefaced with the strongest professions of respect and attachment to this country; of reluctance to enter into any dispute with her; of the readiness you have always shown, and still wish to show, of contributing according to your ability, and in a constitutional way, to her support; and of your determination to undergo every extremity rather than submit to be enslaved. These things tell much in your favour with moderate men, and *with Europe, to whose interposition America may yet owe her salvation,* should the contest be serious and lasting" (Author's emphasis).[39]

Arthur Lee, when the Intolerable Acts were being passed, suddenly decided to go abroad for a few months. Was he in fear of being arrested for treason? Or did he see the futility of protest then and decide to begin negotiating in Europe for aid to the colonists? Before leaving, he wrote on April 2: "There ought to be a general Congress of the Colonies.". . .

Lee's departure left William Bollan, agent for the Massa-

---

*One of the Virginia burgesses who, with Thomas Jefferson and Patrick Henry, gathered at the Raleigh Tavern on May 27, 1774, to denounce the port bill and propose a continental congress.

chusetts Council, the only colonial agent left in London to carry the banner for the colonies. All his efforts—and he made several to present a petition to the two houses of Parliament—were fruitless. Both houses rebuffed him, claiming that he did not have "due Authority to act for the colony," that he was only agent for the Council. A petition from London's American residents, among them Benjamin Franklin, was read to the House of Commons, but to no effect. Similarly, strong appeals from a West Indian merchant, Rose Fuller, and from Edmund Burke were made to an audience of the deaf.

On May 11, the day that Bollan petitioned to be heard by the House of Commons and was rejected, the Duke of Richmond spoke warmly in favor of Boston in the House of Lords, saying that "they [Bostonians] would be in the right to resist, as punished unheard," and, if they did resist, he should wish them success!

The opposition forces in Parliament were weak and divided, outmoded in their thinking. When the Earl of Chatham, the leader of the opposition in the House of Lords, finally appeared, he excused "his late absence by visible tokens of the gout, . . . [having] his legs wrapped in black velvet boots, and as if in mourning for the King of France [who had just died] he leaned on a crutch covered with black. . . . [His] long feeble harangue . . . on one side . . . blamed the violence of the Bostonians, and on the other every step that had provoked them or been taken to chastise them."[40]

Nevertheless, the opposition in the House of Lords entered formal protests on May 11 and 18 against the punitive acts, pointing out the haste with which the acts had been pushed through and the deplorable reliance the government had placed on the military to enforce obedience. The May 11 protest against the bill for the regulation of Massachusetts' government stated in part: "Neither the charter of the colony, nor any account whatever of its courts and judicial proceedings, their mode, or the exercise of their present powers have been produced to the House. The slightest evidence concerning any one of the many inconveniences stated in the Preamble of the Bill to have arisen from the present constitution of the colony judicatures, has not been produced, or even attempted." This protest was signed by 11 members of the House of Lords.

On May 18 a protest against the already passed bill providing for the impartial administration of justice again asserted that no evidence had been laid before the house proving the government's case against the colony. This was signed by eight members of Lords.

Horace Walpole noted that the doors of both houses were locked during the discussions of the bills concerning Boston—"a symptom of the spirit with which they were dictated."

Meanwhile, in America, private letters sent from London in early April were published in the *Boston Gazette* on Monday, May 23, 1774. These letters confirmed Walpole's statement, warning of "an act of Parliament of a most extraordinary kind, to shut up the port of Boston." They went on to say of this act (the Boston Port Bill):

> [It was] . . . smuggled through the House in 17 days only from its introduction. The Evidence before the Privy Council was suppressed, the agents refused a hearing at the bar, and no member for Boston or America in either House. Nor had the merchants and manufacturers in England, who will be deeply affected by the execution of this act, any proper notice of it, or opportunity to remonstrate against it. Indeed it is openly said that many a thousand pounds were issued

from the Treasury to obtain a majority in the House, and hurry it through before there should be time for opposition. So that when a body of merchants trading to Boston and America waited on Lord North with a request that a petition might be heard against the bill, before it passed into a law; they had the mortification to find that they were too late, and that the bill had already passed. As his Majesty has, by the act, a conditional power to suspend its operation, in case the tea destroyed at Boston should be paid for, the merchants offered Lord North £19,000, or a security to the [East] India Company, to pay for the tea, if that suspension of the act might be procured from his Majesty. But these offers were refused, and the merchants went away much dissatisfied—as thinking people are in general, against the proceedings of the Ministry, especially in respect to this law, and the manner of getting it passed, which was with as much privacy and haste as possible so that it is hardly yet known in the manufacturing towns which will be hurt by it.

The writer warned:

It is given out that severe measures are only intended against Boston, to punish their refractory conduct; but depend upon it, if they succeed against Boston, the like measures will be extended to every colony in America; they only begin with Boston, hoping the other colonies will not interpose. But you are all to be visited in turn and devoured one after another. . . . It is a matter of the last importance to them [the colonies] to stand by and support one another; the most favoured can only expect to be last devoured.

The overriding policy of coercion approved by George III and put into execution by Lord North swept all before it. It was far too strong to be stopped by the weak and divided opposition in Parliament.

Having achieved passage of the punitive acts against Massachusetts, Lord North and members of the cabinet and

Parliament left London for their country houses at the end of June.

However, the conscientious Lord Dartmouth was in London to greet Thomas Hutchinson on his arrival and to hurry him off to a two-hour conference with King George on July 1. On July 7 Lord North returned to his official London residence in Downing Street, where he also interviewed Hutchinson. At their meeting, Lord North repeated his strong belief that the rebellious Americans deserved the punitive acts. He regretted only that such measures had not been taken earlier. As he had already told Parliament, "the properest time to exert our right of taxation is when the right is refused."

In early August a disturbing dispatch came to Lord Dartmouth from General Gage: Boston—in fact, the American colonies generally—were planning to resist the punitive acts! They had refused to pay for the tea. So, they were not, after all, going to submit quietly. In an outburst unusual for him, Dartmouth told Hutchinson that he hoped the Boston rebels Hancock and Adams would get the punishment they deserved. Dartmouth feared (Hutchinson reported) that peace would not be restored until some examples were made, in order to forestall other rebellious actions.

Official copies of the punitive acts reached Boston on August 6. The Bostonians stiffened their spines and renewed their appeals to the other colonies for support, repeating that the cause of one was the cause of all. The colonial legislatures and committees of correspondence were busily preparing for the general congress, which was to be known formally as the Continental Congress. That summer, delegates were named and the colonists formulated their ideas as to what the congress should accomplish. It was to convene in Philadelphia on September 1.

On July 6 John Adams, attending circuit court in Falmouth (now Portland), Maine, interrupted a letter to his wife to add in confidence that he must prepare for a "journey to Philadelphia, a long Journey indeed!" Samuel Adams, Robert Treat Paine, Thomas Cushing, and John Adams himself had been chosen as Massachusetts' delegates to the congress—chosen behind locked doors on June 17, just before General Gage, hearing of their business, ordered the dissolution of the Massachusetts House of Representatives.

Gage had written to Lord Dartmouth in July (the dispatch that reached London on August 2) that it was almost impossible for him to bring the tea destroyers to justice, for "tho' I hear of many Things against this and that Person, yet when I . . . want People to stand forth in order to bring Crimes home to Individuals by clear and full Evidence, I am at a Loss." Though he was doing everything in his power to track down the guilty, there was little chance of conviction "at present," Gage reported.

He added that "some of the better Sort of People" had attempted to push through a motion to pay for the destroyed tea in a town meeting, but "they were outvoted by a great Majority of the lower Class."[41]

Although members of the British Government knew by early August that a general congress was to be held in Philadelphia on September 1, scarcely a minister bothered to remain in London. As was usual each summer, the wheels of government in Britain came to a standstill. Lord North told Hutchinson on August 11 (before leaving for the country) that he, for one, did not expect "any great matters from the proposed Congress." Few Britons would have realized or guessed that any great issue, much less the loss of a continent, was at stake—yet the chasm between Britain and the American colonies was rapidly widening.

Not even Hutchinson, though he had adopted the role of counselor to the government in the crisis, could accomplish anything. He wrote to an American, "The present Ministry seem determined not to yield. The body of the people seems to be of the same mind; and if there should be a change of Ministry, of which there is not the least prospect, what can tempt them to new measures?" He believed that if the colonists would pay for the tea and adopt a more resilient, humble attitude, "and . . . advance towards a [more] orderly state than what had been made before I came away," he could obtain "the desired relief for the Bostonians."[42]

Even the news that a considerable quantity of arms for America was being purchased in Holland, caused only a small quiver of alarm in London that summer.

14. *A Congress Meets*

WHAT WAS BRITAIN'S ATTITUDE toward America's prepara- for a general congress?

Hutchinson, in London, said "Nobody seems to give themselves the least concern about the consequences of the projected Congress, supposing it can do no hurt to the Kingdom."[43]

Lord Dartmouth in private hoped that some "tone of accommodation" might arise out of the congress and, if that occurred, he would "think it wise in government to overlook the irregularity of the proceedings, and catch at the opportunity of putting our unhappy differences into some mode of discussion that might save those disagreeable consequences which must arise . . . from open rupture . . . or from . . . interruption of our commercial intercourse with them."[44]

General Gage wrote from Massachusetts on August 27 to inform Dartmouth that the delegates "from this Province are gone to Philadelphia to meet the rest who are to form the General Congress. . . . It is not possible to guess what a Body composed of such heterogeneous Matter will determine, but the Members, from hence, I am assured, will promote the most haughty and insolent Resolves. . . ."[45]

George III at this time was telling Lord North that "The die is now cast, the colonies must either submit or triumph." The King liked to see issues clear-cut.

As often happened with bad news from America, a long letter from General Gage dated September 2 reached London on a Saturday (October 1), when most of the ministers were away.

In his letter Gage despaired of any solution "but by forcible means." The new Crown-appointed councillors were being harassed and forced to resign, he reported. "The flames of sedition had spread universally throughout" Massachusetts. Courts could not function as no jurors would appear. Connecticut and Rhode Island were "as furious as they are in this Province" and all he, Gage, could do was to stabilize his position in Boston, protect the friends of government there, and "reinforce the troops . . . with as many more as could possibly be collected."

The same day that Gage was writing this letter, September 2, the colonists had been alarmed by a report that Gage's troops had removed powder and guns belonging to the local militia from an arsenal in Charlestown. As a result, "a vast concourse" of people, including several thousand armed men, had converged on Cambridge and Boston. It was a show of strength that Gage did not soon forget. He urgently requested additional troops as soon as possible.

He was convinced, he told London, that "the whole is now at stake" and a decisive action must be taken to show the colonies that the government meant what it said and that Britain's laws could not be flouted. In the tone as well as the words of his letter, Gage made it clear that the colonists were not intimidated by the Coercive Acts and would resist. (In late August, Gage had moved his headquarters from Salem to Boston; he had been told that he would be safer there. He was now strengthening his defenses at Boston in every possible way.) Gage claimed that "the late Acts" came too late, should have been adopted seven years ago, and now had "overset the whole, and the Flame blazed out in all Parts at once beyond the Conception of every Body."

Civil government was "near its end" in Boston, he continued, and the rebels were not just "a Boston rabble, but freeholders and farmers." He had written to General Carleton in Quebec to ask for "a body of Canadians and Indians should matters come to extremities."

Clearly Gage was on the verge of panic.

It came as a shock to the British Government that the colonies would resist. Few could believe that the young, raw country "rabble" would actually take on the powerful British Empire. The fact enraged Lord North, who believed that now Parliament could not concede. "It must come to violence."

On September 5, 1774, 55 delegates from 12 of Britain's American colonies met in Philadelphia to consult together on their just grievances and on steps to be taken to bring about repeal of the objectionable acts of Parliament. This was the First Continental Congress. Most of the delegates were instructed by their "constituencies" to seek an accommodation with the parent country.

The "heterogeneous matter" General Gage referred to so contemptuously included some of the best legal and political minds of America—even of the age! There were, for example, "the brace of Adamses" from Massachusetts, John Dickinson of Pennsylvania, John Rutledge of South Carolina, among others. Most of them were meeting their fellow delegates from the other colonies for the first time.

Among those advising the Massachusetts delegates on the goals of the congress was Joseph Hawley of Northampton, Massachusetts. In a lengthy letter to John Adams, he said:

> The Congress ought first to settle with absolute precision the object or objects to be pursued; as whether the end of all shall be the repeal of the tea duty only, or of that and the molasses act, or these and opening the port of Boston, or these and also the restoration of the charter of the Massachussetts Bay. . . . [Then] the means or measures to be used to obtain and effect those ends can be better judged of. . . .
> . . . [the success] of the Congress depends a good deal on the harmony, good understanding, and I had almost said brotherly love, of its members; and every thing tending to beget and improve such mutual affection, and indeed to cement the body, ought to be practised; and every thing in the least tending to create disgust or strangeness, coldness, or so much as indifference, carefully avoided."

Hawley warned Adams that there was an opinion in the other colonies that Massachusetts gentlemen "do affect to dictate and take the lead in continental measures; that we are apt . . . to assume big and haughty airs." Such an impression was to be "most carefully avoided" when meeting the delegates from the other colonies, he solemnly warned.[46]

After careful study of the other members of the congress John Adams wrote on September 8: "There is in the Congress a Collection of the greatest Men upon this Continent, in Point of Abilities, Virtues and Fortunes."[47] He spoke of their magnanimity and public spirit, and he was particularly impressed by the delegates from Virginia, among whom was a wealthy planter named George Washington.

Carpenters' Hall, where the delegates chose to meet, was a new building, barely finished. Appropriately, it was owned and offered for congress' use by a group of mechanics and craftsmen. The 55 delegates must have filled the 18' by 28' room where most of their meetings were held.

The opening of Congress with the reading of the 35th Psalm chosen by the Reverend Jacob Duché, an Episcopal clergyman, had a tremendous effect and set the right tone, according to John Adams. (A rumor that Boston had been bombarded by the British had reached Philadelphia the day before, and the delegates had not yet heard that it was false.) Then the delegates went on to procedural matters and, "with great deliberation," Adams said, the great issues to be discussed. In a rare, confiding moment (for all the delegates took an oath of secrecy) at the close of one of those busy days, Adams wrote his wife "There is no idea of submission here."

Less than two weeks later (on September 17) the congress was considering the resolves of a Suffolk County, Massachusetts, meeting that boldly advocated taking up arms in defense of colonial rights, if it came to that. The text of the resolves had been rushed to the congress in less than five days by Paul Revere on his fast-paced little horse. The Congress endorsed the Suffolk Resolves on the same day they were read.

More weeks of exhaustive discussions ensued, ending on October 26.

What measures taken by the first American congress showed the British Government that its punitive policy had failed? *Twelve colonies had united in a representative body and agreed* that the late acts of Parliament were harsh and unduly oppressive, the foundation "for the utter destruction of American freedom." The congress also adopted a Declaration of Rights and Grievances and proposed a Continental Association. The purpose of the association was to cut off all trade between the colonies and Great Britain until the complained-of acts of Parliament were repealed: therefore, the

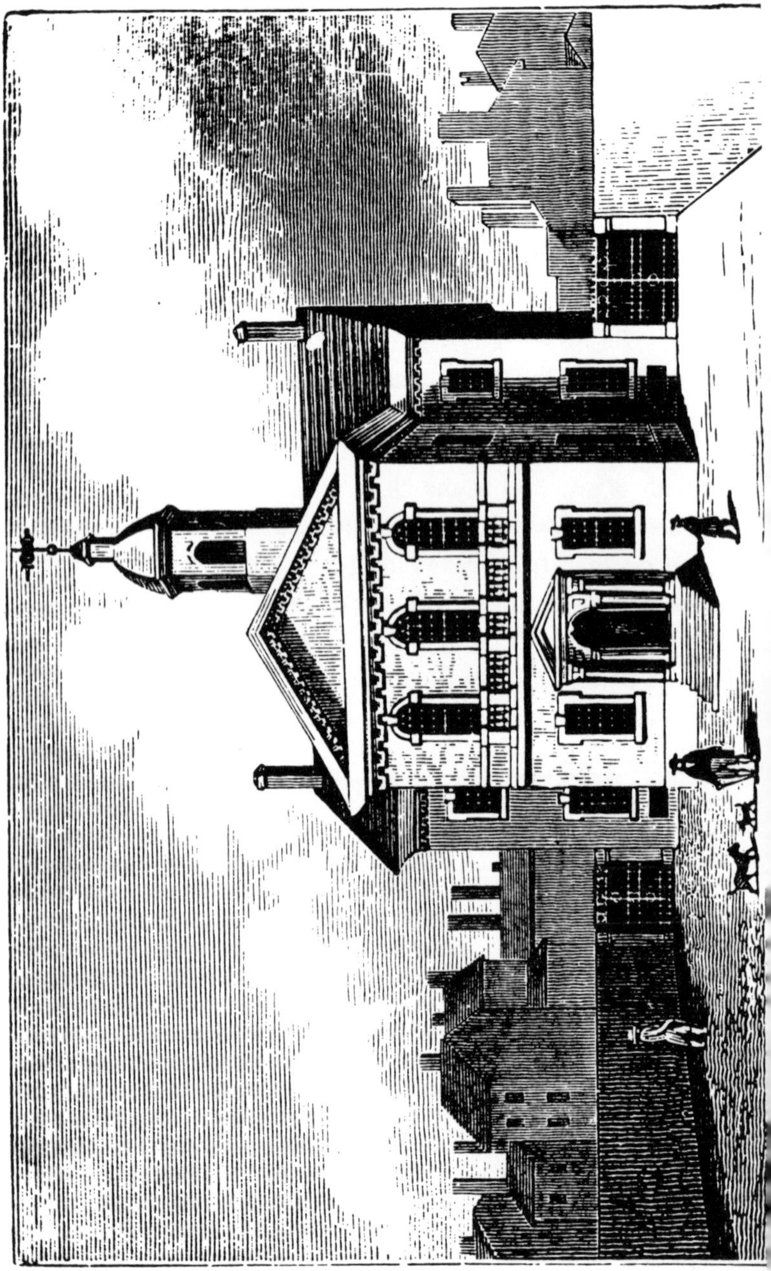

Carpenters' Hall, Philadelphia, where the first Continental Congress met in 1774. Courtesy: Independence National Historical Park Collection.

colonists would cease to import goods from Britain after December 1, 1774, and, as of September 10, 1775, they would cease to export "directly or indirectly . . . any merchandise or commodity whatsoever to Great Britain, Ireland, or the West Indies, except rice to Europe." The boycott would be enforced by local committees of inspection.

The colonists hoped that, as before, the economic pinch would force the repeal of the obnoxious British legislation, and that the threat to Britain's trade would arouse a response from her citizenry. It did. But so did the drilling of thousands of colonial militia men and the realization that Gage and his troops were virtually prisoners in Boston—until more military might could be sent there.

Although the delegates repeatedly expressed their loyalty to the King (not realizing his strong opposition to their cause), they wished for the support of all the people of Great Britain, Canada, the British West Indies and all other parts of the empire. Struggling for the ancient rights of Britons, many colonists felt that they were fighting on behalf of all Englishmen.

In transmitting the congress's address to the King and its memorial to the British people, Charles Thomson, the secretary of the congress, hoped the documents would show that "it is not a little faction, but the whole of American freeholders from Nova Scotia to Georgia that now complain and apply for redress." (Unfortunately, neither Nova Scotia nor Georgia were represented in Congress; both were Tory strongholds. Georgia at the time needed British troops to defend her people against an Indian uprising.)

"The first Congress advertised the growing strength of radical feeling. . . . The first Continental Congress was many things: it was a clearing house for discontent and a united voice for the member Colonies; it was an act of rebellion against the old Empire and the seedbed of a federal union in the New World. Above all it was a challenge to George III and his Ministers, for it set America against Great Britain."[48] This is the opinion of a 20th-century British historian.

The First Continental Congress adjourned on October 26, 1774, resolving to meet the following spring if conditions warranted. Within six months after its adjournment, each of the colonies that had participated approved many of its actions.[49]

Maryland, for example, held a convention at Annapolis in December 1774 that was typical of others throughout the land. There, "the proceedings of the continental congress were read, considered, and unanimously approved. *Resolved,* That every member of this convention will, and every person in the province ought, strictly and inviolably to observe and carry into execution the [Continental] association agreed on by the said continental congress." Marylanders went on to resolve: "[to] increase our flocks of sheep, and thereby promote the woolen manufacture in this province . . . to increase the manufacture of linen and cotton &c." They also resolved, unanimously, "That a well regulated militia . . . is the natural strength and only stable security of a free government, and that such militia will relieve our mother country from any expense in our protection and defence; will obviate the pretence of a necessity for taxing us on that account, and render it unnecessary to keep any standing army (ever dangerous to liberty) in this province." Therefore, the Maryland men between the ages of 16 and 50 would form themselves into militia companies and "use their utmost endeavors" to make themselves masters of the military exercise. "Each man [would] be provided with a good firelock and bayonet fitted thereon, half a pound of powder, two pounds of lead, and a cartouch-box, or powder-horn and a bag for ball, and be in readiness to act on any emergency."[50]

By the end of 1774 many Americans were prepared to defend and protect "their lives, fortunes and sacred honor" with powder and ball if need be.

In response to General Gage's September request, the British Admiralty sent three guardships from home ports with ten companies of marines that reached Boston in early December 1774. These were the marines under Major Pitcairn whom Gage sent the following spring to Lexington and Concord to capture military stores. There they fired upon the colonial militia and were themselves fired upon. Blood was shed, and the horrors of a "civil war" were begun.

Appendix I

Was the destruction of the tea necessary?

The ablest and best informed lawyer of the place and time, John Adams, asked himself that question and wrote the answer in his diary:

> I apprehend it was absolutely and indispensably so. They could not send it back, the Governor, Admiral and Collector and Comptroller would not suffer it. It was in their Power to have saved it—but in no other. It could not get by the Castle, The Men of War &c. Then there was no other Alternative but to destroy it or let it be landed. To let it be landed, would be giving up the Principle of Taxation by Parliamentary Authority, against which the Continent have struggled for 10 years, it was losing all our labour for 10 years and subjecting ourselves and our Posterity forever to Egyptian taskmasters—to Burthens [Burdens], Indignities, to Ignominy, Reproach and Contempt, to Desolation and Oppression, to Poverty and Servitude.
> But it will be said it might have been left in the Care of a Committee of the Town, or in Castle William [on Castle Island]. To this many Objections may be made . . . the Tories blame the Consignees, as much as the Whiggs do—[51]

Who were the "Indians" who tossed the tea into Boston Harbor?

"They were no ordinary Mohawks," wrote John Adams. Perhaps most of the "Indians" who boarded the tea ships and broke open the chests and threw away the tea knew one another; and later, after all danger was past, many a person claimed to have known or been one of them. But their true identities remained a well-kept secret. The nucleus of the tribe was very likely the citizens' watch that was set on the tea ships on November 29, but any records of the members of this watch, which changed from time to time during this critical period, were carefully destroyed.

John Adams later recalled that he had taken special pains *not* to be told or to learn who the "Indians" were, for he "expected every day an indictment" against them "and that [I] should be called upon to defend them in a court of justice."

Was the destruction of the tea a "riot"?

Every precaution was taken by those in charge of the citizens' meetings to make sure that no riot occurred. According to one eyewitness, Hugh Williamson, the tea meetings were conducted with all the dignity of "the British Senate." No one sought to violate any of the laws applying to the tea *except* the Townshend tax against which the citizens had been long protesting. The various newspaper accounts agreed that the tea's destruction was carried out with precision and dispatch and that no other goods were damaged. As the *Massachusetts Gazette* of December 23 stated:

> It is worthy of remark that although a considerable quantity of goods were still remaining on board the vessel

no injury was sustained. Such attention to private property was observed that a small padlock belonging to the captain of one of the ships being broke, another was procured and sent to him. The town was very quiet during the whole evening and the night following. Those who were from the country went home with a merry heart, and the next day joy appeared in almost every countenance, some on account of the destruction of the tea, others on account of the quietness with which it was effected.

Throughout the tea party, no violence was done to any of the customs men, nor to their houses or other property. The only person who was at all roughly handled was an Irishman who was discovered trying to secrete some of the tea in the lining of his coat.

Appendix II

AN EYEWITNESS wrote the following account of the tea meetings in Boston, published in the *Boston Gazette* of December 20, 1773, and signed "An Impartial Observer." The author has not been identified by name, but this account nonetheless reveals that he was a Rhode Islander in sympathy with the Boston patriots.

Having accidentally arrived at Boston upon a visit to a Friend, the Evening before the meeting of the body of the People on the 29th of November, curiosity and the pressing invitation of my kind host induced me to attend the meeting. I must confess I was so agreeably, and I hope I shall be forgiven by this people if I say so unexpectedly entertained and instructed by the regular, reasonable, and sensible conduct of the people there collected, that I should rather have entertained an idea of being transported to the British senate than to an adventitious and promiscuous assembly of people of a remote Colony, were I not convinced by the genuine uncorrupted integrity and manly hardihood of the Rhetoricians of that Assembly, that they were not yet corrupted by venality or debauched by luxury. The conduct of that wise and considerate body in their several transactions evidently tended to preserve the property of the East India Company: I must confess I was very disagreeably affected with the conduct of Mr. Hutchinson, their pensioned Governor, on the suceeding day, who very unseasonably, and as I am informed, very arbitrarily (not having the sanction of law) framed and executed a Mandate to disperse the people, which in my opinion, with a people less prudent and temperate, would have cost him his head: The force of that body was directed to effect the return of the Teas to Great Britain; much argument was expended; much entreaty was made use of to effect this desirable purpose. Mr. Rotch behaved in my estimation very unexceptionably; his disposition was seemingly to comport with the desires of the people to convey the Teas to the original proprietors. The Consignees have behaved like Scoundrels in refusing to take the consignment, or indemnify the owner of the ship which conveyed this detestable commodity to this port; every possible step was taken to preserve this property; the people, being exasperated with the conduct of administration in this affair, great pains were taken, and much policy exerted to procure a stated watch* for this purpose. The body of the people determined the Tea should not be landed; the determination was deliberate, was judicious; the sacrifice of their Rights, of the Union of all the Colonies, would have been the effect, had they conducted with less resolution. On the Committee of Correspondence they devolved the care of seeing their resolutions seasonably executed; that body, as I have been informed by one of their members, had taken every step which prudence and patriotism could suggest, to effect the desirable purpose, but were defeated.

The Body once more assembled, I was again present;

*This watch consisted of 24 to 34 men, who served as volunteers 19 days and 23 hours.

such a collection of the people was to me a novelty; near seven thousand persons from several towns, Gentlemen, Merchants, Yeomen and others respectable for their rank and abilities, and venerable for their age and character, constituted the assembly; they decently, unanimously and firmly adhered to their former resolution, that a baleful commodity which was to rivet & establish the duty should never be landed; to prevent the mischief, they repeated the desires of the committee of the towns that the owner of the ship should apply for a clearance; it appeared that Mr. Rotch had been managed and was still under the influence of the opposite party; he refused the request of the people to apply for a clearance for his ship with an obstinacy which in my opinion bordered on stubbornness—subdued at length by the peremptory demand of the Body, he consented to apply, a committee of ten respectable gentlemen were appointed to attend him to the collector. The succeeding morning the application was made and a clearance refused with all the insolence of office; the Body meeting the same morning by adjournment, Mr. Rotch was directed to protest in form, and then apply to the Governor for a Pass by the castle; Mr. Rotch executed his commission with fidelity, but a pass could not be obtained, his Excellency excusing himself in his refusal that he should not make the precedent of granting a pass till the clearance was obtained; which was indeed a fallacy as it had been usual with him in ordinary cases. Mr. Rotch returning in the evening reported as above; the Body then voted his conduct to be satisfactory, and recommending order and regularity to the people, Dissolved.

Previous to the dissolution, a number of persons, supposed to be the Aboriginal Natives from their complection, approaching near the door of the assembly, gave the War Whoop, which was answered by a few in the galleries of the house where the assembly was convened; silence was commanded, and a prudent and peaceable deportment again enjoined. The Savages repaired to the ships which entertained the pestilential Teas, and had begun their rampage (?) previous to the dissolution of the meeting————————They applied themselves to the destruction of this commodity in earnest and in the space of about two hours broke up 342 chests, and discharged their contents into the sea. A watch, as I am informed, was stationed to prevent embezzlement, and not a single ounce of Tea was suffered to be purloined or carried off.

It is worthy remark that, although a considerable quantity of goods of different kinds were still remaining on board the vessels, no injury was sustained; such attention to private property was observed that a small padlock belonging to the Capt. of one of the ships being broke, another was procured and sent to him.——————————I cannot but express my admiration at the conduct of this people! Uninfluenced by party or any other attachment, I presume I shall not be suspected of misrepresentation.

The East India Company must console themselves with this . . . that, if they have suffered, the prejudice they sustain does not arise from enmity to them: a fatal necessity has rendered this catastrophe inevitable—the landing (of) the tea would have been fatal, as it would have saddled the colonies with a duty imposed without their consent & which no power on earth can effect. Their strength, numbers, spirit and illumination render the experiment dangerous, the defeat certain: The Consignees must attribute to themselves the loss of the property of the East India Company. Had they seasonably quieted the minds of the people by a resignation, all had been well. The custom house and the man who disgraces majesty by representing him, acting in confederacy with the inveterate enemies of America, stupidly opposed every measure concerted to return the teas.

That American virtue may defeat every attempt to enslave them, is the warmest wish of my heart. I shall return home doubly fortified in my resolution to prevent that deprecated calamity, the landing the teas in Rhode Island, and console myself with the happiest assurances that my brethren have not less virtue, less resolution than their neighbours.

An Impartial Observer.

Appendix III

THE FOLLOWING LETTER* is of special interest, for it was written from Boston, December 31, 1773, by Samuel Adams, who is often regarded as the chief instigator of the "tumults" in Boston. It was sent to Arthur Lee in London.

My dear Sir:

I am now to inform you of as remarkable an event as has yet happened since the commencement of our struggle for American liberty. The meeting of the town of Boston, an account of which I enclosed in my last, was succeeded by the arrival of the ship Falmouth,† Captain Hall, with 114 chests of the East India Company's tea, on the 28th of November last. The next day the people met in Faneuil hall, without observing the rules prescribed by law for calling them together; and although that hall is capable of holding 1200 or 1300 men, they were soon obliged for the want of room to adjourn to the Old South meeting-house; where were assembled upon this important occasion 5000, some say 6000 men,

---

*From Harry Alonzo Cushing, ed., *The Writings of Samuel Adams* (New York, G. P. Putnam's, 1904, 1908).

†Adams wrote "Falmouth," but the ship was the *Dartmouth*, as described above.

consisting of the respectable inhabitants of this and the adjacent towns. The business of the meeting was conducted with decency, unanimity, and spirit. Their resolutions you will observe in an enclosed printed paper. It naturally fell upon the correspondence [committee] for the town of Boston to see that these resolutions were carried into effect. This committee, finding that the owner of the ship after she was unloaded of all her cargo except the tea, was by no means disposed to take the necessary steps for her sailing back to London, thought it best to call in the committees of Charlestown, Cambridge, Brookline, Roxbury, and Dorchester, all of which towns are in the neighbourhood of this, for their advice and assistance. After a free conference and due consideration, they dispersed. The next day being the 14th, inst. the people met again at the Old South church, and having ascertained the owner, they *compelled* him to apply at the custom house for a clearance for his ship to London with the tea on board, and appointed ten gentlemen to see it performed; after which they adjourned till Thursday the 16th. The people then met, and Mr. Rotch informed them that he had according to their injunction applied to the collector of the customs for a clearance, and received in answer from the collector that he could not consistently with his duty grant him a clearance, until the ship should be discharged of the dutiable article on board. It must be here observed that Mr. Rotch had before made a tender of the tea to the consignees, being told by them that it was not practicable for them at that time to receive the tea, by reason of a constant guard kept upon it by armed men; but that when it might be practicable, they would receive it. He demanded the captain's bill of lading and the freight, both which they refused him, against which he entered a regular protest. The people then required Mr. Rotch to protest the refusal of the collector to grant him a clearance under these circumstances, and thereupon to wait upon the governor for a permit to pass the castle in her voyage to London, and then adjourned till the afternoon. They then met, and after waiting till sun-setting, Mr. Rotch returned, and acquainted them that the governor had refused to grant him a passport, thinking it inconsistent with the laws and his duty to the king, to do it until the ship should be qualified, notwithstanding Mr. Rotch had acquainted him with the circumstances above mentioned. You will observe by the printed proceedings, that the people were resolved that the tea should not be landed, but sent back to London in the same bottom; and the property should be safe guarded while in port, which they punctually performed. It cannot therefore be fairly said that the destruction of the property was in their contemplation. It is proved that the consignees, together with the collector of the customs, and the governor of the province, prevented the safe return of the East India Company's property (the danger of the sea only excepted) to London. The people finding all their endeavours for this purpose thus totally frustrated, dissolved the meeting, which had consisted by common estimation of at least seven thousand men, many of whom had come from towns at the distance of twenty miles. In less than four hours every chest of tea on board three ships which had by this time arrived, *three hundred and forty-two chests,* or rather the contents of them, was thrown into the sea, without the least injury to the vessels or any other property. The only remaining vessel which was expected with this detested article, is by the act of righteous heaven cast on shore on the back of Cape Cod, which has often been the sad fate of many a more valuable cargo. For a more particular detail of facts, I refer you to our worthy friend, Dr. Hugh Williamson, who kindly takes the charge of this letter. We have had great pleasure in his company for a few weeks past; and he favoured the meeting with his presence.

You cannot imagine the height of joy that sparkles in the eyes and animates the countenances as well as the hearts of all we meet on this occasion; excepting the disappointed, disconcerted Hutchinson and his tools. I repeat what I wrote you in my last; if lord Dartmouth has prepared his plan let him produce it speedily; but his lordship must know that it must be such a plan as will not barely amuse, much less farther irritate but conciliate the affection of the inhabitants.

I had forgot to tell you that before the arrival of either of these ships, the tea commissioners had preferred a petition to the governor and council, praying "to resign themselves and the property in their care, to his excellency and the board as guardians and protectors of the people, and that measures may be directed for the landing and securing the tea," &c. I have enclosed you the result of the council on that petition. He (the governor) is now, I am told, consulting *his* lawyers and books to make out that the resolves of the meeting are treasonable. I duly received your favours of the 23d June, of the 21st July and 13th October, and shall make the best use I can of the important contents.

Believe me to be affectionately your friend,

Samuel Adams

Notes

1. James K. Hosmer, *The Life of Thomas Hutchinson* (Boston and New York: Houghton, Mifflin and Company, 1896).
2. A. Francis Steuart, ed., *The Last Journals of Horace Walpole During the Reign of George III from 1771-1783,* 2 vols. (London: John Lane, 1910), vol. I, p. 72.
3. From a letter written by Franklin to Samuel Cooper, July 7, 1773, as quoted in Jared Sparks, *Works of Franklin,* 10 vols. (Chicago: T. McCoun, 1882).
4. From a letter written by Hutchinson, October 3, 1770, quoted in Hosmer, *Life of Thomas Hutchinson,* p. 197.
5. From a letter by an unnamed British officer, as quoted in *Traits of the Tea Party: being a Memoir of George R. T. Hewes, one of the last of its survivors; with a History of that Transaction; Reminiscences of the Massacre, and the Siege, and Other Stories of Old Times. By a Bostonian.* (New York: Harper & Brothers, 1835).
6. Resolutions of Philadelphians, as quoted in David Ramsay, *History of the United States,* 3 vols. (Philadelphia: M. Carey and Son, 1818).
7. From letter of Thomas Hutchinson, November 15, 1773, no. 570 in Massachusetts Archives.
8. From a letter written by Hutchinson to Richard Jackson, August 30, 1765, as quoted in Hosmer, *Life of Thomas Hutchinson,* pp. 92-93.
9. From a letter written by Hutchinson to Lord Dart-

mouth, October 9, 1773, as quoted in James K. Hosmer, *Samuel Adams* (Boston and New York: Houghton Mifflin Company, 1885), pp. 240-242.
10. From a letter written by Hutchinson to William Palmer, in London, August 7, 1773, in Massachusetts Archives.
11. Thomas Hutchinson, *The History of the Province of Massachusetts Bay,* ed. by Lawrence Shaw Mayo, 3 vols. (Cambridge, Mass.: Harvard University Press, 1936), pp. 303-304.
12. From a letter written by Henry Pelham in Boston, to Charles Pelham, November 5, 1773. Copley-Pelham Letters, in Massachusetts Historical Society.
13. From a letter written by Hutchinson, in Milton, to an unnamed friend, November 24, 1773, in Massachusetts Archives. Also quoted in *Massachusetts Historical Society Proceedings* (hereafter cited as *MHSP*) (December 1873), p. 166.
14. Selectmen's Minutes, November 27-28, 1773. City Document no. 42.
15. *Boston Gazette,* November 22, 1773.
16. The fourth Boston-bound tea ship, the brigantine *William,* was wrecked on Cape Cod on December 10, 1773. However, her cargo of 58 chests of tea and 300 street lamps (Boston's first) was salvaged. The patriots were dismayed to learn that most of this tea was secretly conveyed to Castle Island through the efforts of Jonathan Clarke. Presumably this tea was sold to and consumed by loyalists. But there is no record of the duty on this shipment ever having been paid. The minutes of meetings of the Boston selectmen reveal the care with which the tea on the *Beaver* was handled. On December 8, the selectmen directed the keeper of the hospital on Rainsford Island (where the *Beaver* was being detained because of a smallpox outbreak on board) to "take the whole of the Tea from between Decks upon the Deck of the Briggandine. If the Weather be fair, let it lay on the Deck the whole Day to be aired, and at Night see it put between Decks again, and you with the two Men you are ordered to take down with you are to remain on board during the time the Tea is on Deck and

on no account to absent yourselves, and by no means suffer one chest of Tea to be landed or taken away by any one. If any attempt should be made, you are immediately to dispatch a Messenger to inform the Selectmen thereof." The other articles in the cargo were to be taken on shore to be cleansed. As soon as this was done, the keeper was to report to the selectmen who would then issue orders "for the Vessels coming to Town."

17. As quoted in Samuel Lane Boardman, ed., *Peter Edes, Pioneer Printer in Maine* (Bangor: 1901).
18. *MHSP* (December 1873), p. 197.
19. From report of an eyewitness, said to be a "moderate Tory," in "Proceedings of Ye Body Respecting the Tea" by L. F. S. Upton, *William & Mary Quarterly* (1965).
20. Anne Rowe Cunningham, ed., *Letters and Diary of John Rowe* (Boston: W. B. Clarke Company, 1903).
21. From a letter written by Hutchinson to ex-governor Francis Bernard, January 1, 1774, as quoted in *MHSP* (December 1873), p. 174.
22. From a letter written by Hutchinson to James Warren. December 17, 1773, as quoted in Charles Francis Adams, ed., *The Works of John Adams*, 10 vols. (Boston: Little, Brown & Co., 1850-56). And in his letter of December 22 Adams told Warren: "The spirit of liberty is very high in the country, and universal. Worcester is aroused. . . . A gentleman of as good sense and character as any in that county, told me this day, that nothing which has been ever done, is more universally approved, applauded, and admired than these last efforts. He says, that whole towns in that county were on tiptoe to come down."
23. Lyman H. Butterfield, et. al., eds., *Diary and Autobiography of John Adams* (Cambridge, Mass.: Harvard University Press, 1961).
24. Hutchinson, *History*, p. 315.
25. *Diary . . . of John Adams.*
26. From a letter written by Thomas Hutchinson Jr. to his brother Elisha, as quoted in P. O. Hutchinson, ed., *Diary and Letters of Thomas Hutchinson, Esq.,* 2 vols.

(London: Sampson Low, Marston, Searle & Rivington, 1886).
27. *Ibid.*
28. From a letter written by Hutchinson to Lord Dartmouth, in Massachusetts Archives.
29. *Ibid.*
30. As described in John Bigelow, comp. and ed., *The Works of Benjamin Franklin* (New York and London: G. P. Putnam's, 1904), Vol. VI, p. 297.
31. From a letter written by Thomas Gage to Thomas Hutchinson, February 2, 1774, as quoted in *Diary and Letters of Hutchinson,* Vol. I, p. 100.
32. Mrs. Paget Toynbee, ed., *The Letters of Horace Walpole, Fourth Earl of Oxford* (Oxford, Eng.: Clarendon Press, 1904), Vol. VIII, pp. 418-419.
33. W. Baring Pemberton, *Lord North* (London: Longmans Green & Co., Ltd., 1938). Courtesy of The Longman Group Ltd.
34. Mercy Otis Warren, *History of the Rise, Progress and Termination of the American Revolution,* 3 vols. (Boston: E. Larkin, 1805), Vol. I, p. 107.
35. William Cobbett, ed., *The Parliamentary History of England* (London: Hansard, 1806-20).
36. Charles Francis Adams, ed., *Correspondence of John Adams* (Boston: Little, Brown & Co., 1850-56), p. 337.
37. From John Andrews' Diary, in *MHSP* (July 1865).
38. From a letter written by Franklin, February 2, 1774, as quoted in *Transactions of The Colonial Society of Massachusetts* (Boston: The Colonial Society of Massachusetts, 1902), vol. 5, p. 57.
39. From a letter written by Arthur Lee, in London, to his brother, Richard H. Lee, in America, March 18, 1774, as quoted in Peter Force, ed., *American Archives: Fourth Series* (Washington, 1837, 1839).
40. Steuart, *Last Journals of Horace Walpole,* vol. 1, pp. 344, 347-49.
41. C. E. Carter, ed., *The Correspondence of General Thomas Gage With the Secretaries of State, 1763-1775*

(New Haven: Yale University Press, 1931-33), pp. 367, 374.
42. From a letter written by Hutchinson, in London, to an unnamed American, August 9, 1774, as quoted in *Diary and Letters of Hutchinson.*
43. From a letter written by Thomas Hutchinson, in London, to one of his sons, August 1774, as quoted in *Diary and Letters of Hutchinson,* vol. 1, p. 221.
44. From a letter written by Lord Dartmouth to Hardwicke, August 29, 1774, as quoted in Bernard Donoughue, *British Politics and the American Revolution* (London: Macmillan & Co., 1964). [From the Hardwicke Papers in the British Museum.] New York: St. Martin's Press, 1964.
45. *Correspondence of Thomas Gage.*
46. From a letter written by Joseph Hawley to John Adams, July 25, 1774, as quoted in *The Works of John Adams,* Vol. IX, pp. 342-346.
47. L. H. Butterfield, Wendell D. Garrett, and Marjorie E. Sprage, eds., *Adams Family Correspondence* (Cambridge, Mass.: The Belknap Press of Harvard University Press, 1963), vol. 1, p. 150.
48. Donoughue, *British Politics and the American Revolution,* pp. 173-174.
49. Although New York as a whole did not approve the Continental Association, local committees of inspection were active in some of its counties. In Georgia, 45 delegates attended a provincial congress on March 18, 1775, and ratified the association.
50. Report of the meeting held at Annapolis, Maryland, in December 1774, in Alden T. Vaughn, ed., *Chronicles of the American Revolution* (New York: Grosset & Dunlap, 1965).
51. Diary entry for December 17, 1773, as quoted in *Diary of John Adams.*

Reading List

FLEXNER, JAMES THOMAS. *The Double Adventures of John Copley.* Boston: Little, Brown and Company, 1969. [The famous painter's role as a mediator in the tea dispute is narrated in Chapter 7.]

FORBES, ESTHER. *Paul Revere and the World He Lived in.* Boston: Houghton Mifflin Company, 1942.

FRANKENSTEIN, ALFRED. *The World of Copley, 1738-1815.* New York: Time-Life Books, 1970.

LABAREE, BENJAMIN WOODS. *The Boston Tea Party.* New York: Oxford University Press, 1964.

MILLER, HELEN HILL. *The Case for Liberty.* Chapel Hill: University of North Carolina Press, 1965.

MORGAN, EDMUND S. and HELEN M. *The Stamp Act Crisis: Prologue to Revolution.* Chapel Hill: University of North Carolina Press, 1953.

OLIVER, PETER. *Origin and Progress of the American Rebellion: A Tory View.* Edited by Douglass Adair and John A. Schutz. Stanford, Cal.: Stanford University Press, 1961.

PLUMB, J. H. *England in the Eighteenth Century (1714-1815).* A Pelican Original. Baltimore: Penguin Books, 1950. [See Part II, The Age of Chatham.]

———. *Men and Centuries.* Boston: Houghton Mifflin Company, 1963. [Useful for a view of British life during the 18th century, particularly among the upper classes.]

RICHMOND, ROBERT P. *Powder Alarm 1774.* Princeton, N.J.: Auerbach Publishers Inc., 1971. [A succinct account of the raid on the powderhouse at Charlestown, Mass., mentioned in this volume.]

Index

Active (ship) 56
Acts of Trade 57
Adams, John 1, 21, 66-67, 72, 97, 110, 115, 116, 117
Adams, Samuel 5, 8, 11, 20, 27, 29-30, 35, 42, 51, 60, 66, 68, 69, 86, 87, 91, 97, 99-100, 101, 109, 110, 115
Alarm (news broadside) 23
Andrews, John 101
Assembly: *see* General Court
Avery, John Jr. 8

Banbury, Oxon 85
Bass, Henry 8
Bath, Somersetshire, Eng. 85
Beacon Hill, Boston 51
Beaver (ship) 40, 42, 52, 61
Bengal 81
Bernard, Francis 5, 66, 87
Bill of Rights 100
Body meetings 50, 52-53, 55-61, 63, 66, 68, 89, 91
  Governor's message to 51
Bollan, William 104-106
Boston 1, 2, 5, 13, 17, 21, 23, 25, 26, 34, 39, 40, 43, 73, 100, 106, 117
  circular letter 20, 35, 99
  committee of correspondence 20, 44, 72, 89, 91, 98
  merchants 101
  military alert 51
  punishment 80-81, 92-96, 106, 108

  selectmen 26, 40, 43-44, 50, 56, 66, 89
  support from other colonies 68, 100
Boston Gazette 33, 40, 45, 48, 72, 99, 107
Boston Harbor 28, 42-44, 52, 60, 93, 98, 102
Boston Massacre 67, 96, 100
Boston Port Bill 93-95, 97-102, 104, 105, 107
Boston Tea Party 19, 68, 72, 104
  eyewitnesses 77, 89
  reactions 66-73, 78-81, 95
  ringleaders 98, 110
  second tea party 73
Boston town meeting 2, 3, 30, 41, 95, 97-98, 102
Bostonians 1, 8, 24, 41, 43, 47, 48, 81, 94, 97, 106, 111
Bowdoin family 26
Brattle, William 67
Britain 87, 98, 99, 110, 120-121
  Admiralty 122
  constitution 2, 8
  crown appointees 2, 20, 95, 114
  empire 4, 81, 115, 120-121
  exchequer 4, 11, 83
  government 6, 12, 24, 29, 42, 68, 79, 87, 94, 110, 115, 117
  liberties 7, 8, 11, 15
  mercantile policy 3
  merchants 3, 9, 10, 19, 30, 104, 107, 108
  ministry 24, 34, 67, 80, 87, 101, 102, 108, 111

145

navy 3, 7, 43
subjects' rights 11, 120
troops 11, 18, 43, 56, 63, 67, 81, 96, 98, 114, 120
warships 42, 43, 52, 56, 63
Bruce, James 40, 66
Burke, Edmund 103, 106
Bushey Park, Middlesex, Eng. 85

Cambridge, Mass. 44, 67-68, 114
Canada 4, 120
Carpenters' Hall 116-117
Castle Island 28, 30, 42, 43, 52, 56, 63, 68, 72-74, 88
Chancellor of the exchequer 11
Charleston, S.C. 40, 69, 88
Charlestown, Mass. 44, 69, 114
Chase, Thomas 8
Chatham, Earl of (William Pitt) 106
Church, Benjamin 40, 66, 91
Churchill, Winston 86
Clarke & Sons 24, 40, 43
Clarke family 26, 40, 88
Clarke, Jonathan 43-44, 74
Clarke, Richard 40, 43
Cleverly, Stephen 8
Coffin, Hezekiah 40
Coke, Edward 1
Colerain, Mass. 72
Colonies
  agents in London 6-7, 103, 104, 107
  charters 7
  governors 24
  legislatures 2, 6, 10, 20, 109
  manufactures 3, 12, 121
  militia 21, 120, 121-122
  shipping 3, 7
  trade 3, 35, 51-52
Colonies, American 19, 103, 110, 114
  merchants 3-4, 8-9, 10, 12, 13, 19, 34, 38
  prosperity 3-4
  southern colonies 3
  support of Boston 68, 100, 109
  taxation 4

threat to 108
unite 9, 10, 68, 100, 117, 121
Committee for Tarring and Feathering 73
Committees of correspondence 20, 35, 44, 68, 105, 109
Committee of the Privy Council for Plantation Affairs 78
Commons, House of 10, 12, 85, 86, 94, 103, 106
Communications 24, 28, 29
Conciliation efforts 10, 103, 104, 106, 111, 115
Concord, Mass. 122
Congress, Continental (First) 69, 99-101, 105, 109-110, 113-122
  delegates 109-110, 113, 115-117
Connecticut 114
Connecticut River 72
Cooper, William 66
Crafts, Thomas 8
Cushing, Thomas 18, 66, 101, 110
Customs commissioners 11
Customs officers 4, 6-7, 13, 43, 49, 52, 55, 91-93
Customs system 4, 49

Dalton, Michael 1
Dartmouth, Mass. 40
Dartmouth (ship) 40, 42, 43, 47, 50-56, 61
  clearance refused 56-57
Dartmouth, Earl of (William Legge) 18, 29, 30, 75, 77-78, 83, 91, 92, 102, 105, 109, 110, 113
Declaration of Rights and Grievances 117
Declaratory Act 11
Delaware 10
Delaware River 41
Denny, William 40, 91
Dickinson, John 10, 13, 23, 87, 115
Dillington, Somersetshire, Eng. 83, 85
Dolphin (ship) 77
Dorchester, Mass. 44
Duché, Jacob 117

INDEX

East India Company 13-15, 19, 21-23, 30-31, 33-35, 38-39, 43, 44, 48-49, 77-78, 79, 85, 93, 100, 101, 104, 108
East India Tea Act 19, 21, 24, 33-34, 86
  resistance to 24, 33-35, 38, 43-45, 47, 49, 57, 60-61, 69
Edes & Gill 33, 74
Edes, Benjamin 8, 57
Edes, Peter 57
Eleanor (ship) 40, 42, 52, 61, 63, 66
Embargo 9, 117
English colonies in America: *see* Colonies, American
Erving, George 101
Eton College 83
Europe 1, 14, 83, 86, 101, 105, 120

Faneuil, Benjamin 40, 44, 74
Faneuil Hall 38, 39, 40, 44-45, 47, 97, 102
Faneuil family 26
Fifth of November 34, 39
Financial crisis 14
Fort William 28, 30, 43
Fortune (ship) 73
France 3
  colonies 3, 4
  king 106
Franklin, Benjamin 17-19, 29, 72, 78-80, 103-106
  on tea party 79, 101
French and Indian War 3
Fuller, Rose 106

Gage, Thomas 80-81, 96, 98, 102, 109, 110, 113, 120, 122
  requests more troops 114-115
General Court 2, 11, 20-21, 26, 29, 30, 48, 101
George III 10, 15, 77, 80, 85, 92, 103, 104, 108-109, 114, 121
  colonies petition 10, 15, 18, 120
Georgia 10, 120
Gibbon, Edward 86

Governor's Council 2, 23, 28, 29, 30, 42, 47-48, 67-68, 90, 92, 95, 96, 106, 114
Gravesend 77
Great Britain: *see* Britain
Green Dragon Tavern 57
Grenville, George 4
Gridley, Jeremiah 1
Griffin's Wharf 19, 50, 52, 55, 57, 61
Gunpowder Plot 39
Guy Fawkes Day 34, 39

Halifax, Nova Scotia 4, 42
Hall, James 40, 43, 47, 50
Hallowell, Benjamin 53
Hancock, John 41, 51, 66, 77, 92, 100, 101, 109
Harmony (ship) 97
Harrison, Richard 53
Harvard College 26, 28
Hawley, Joseph 115-116
Hayley (ship) 77
Henry, Patrick 7, 10, 105
History of the Colony and Province of Massachusetts Bay, The 28, 62, 102
Holland 13, 111
Horace (quotation) 76
House of Commons: *see* Commons, House of
House of Lords: *see* Lords, House of
House of Representatives 2, 17-18, 21, 26, 78, 95, 104, 110
Hutchinson, Anne 25
Hutchinson, Elisha 23, 24, 30, 40, 73-75, 102
Hutchinson-Oliver letters 17-19, 72, 75, 78-79
Hutchinson, Peggy 28, 102
Hutchinson, Thomas 5, 13, 14, 20-21, 23, 24, 34, 38, 39, 40, 41-43, 47-48, 50, 51, 52, 55, 56, 60, 63, 66-68, 75-76, 79, 80, 86, 87, 89, 94, 103, 105, 109, 110, 113
  biography 25-31
  criticism of 21, 29, 51, 75

petition for removal of 18-19, 75, 78
replaced 81, 102
report of tea party 77, 89-90
represented by solicitor general 78
role in England 111
Hutchinson, Thomas, Jr. 23, 24, 30, 40, 73-75

Impartial Administration of Justice Act 95, 107
Impressment of Americans by British navy 7
Independence 29, 80, 92-93, 102, 104
India 4, 14, 19
Indians 57, 60-61, 72, 74, 89, 115, 120
Inns of Court 1
Intolerable Acts 94-96, 98, 100, 105, 106-109
 colonies resist 109, 114
Ireland 120

James I 7
Jefferson, Thomas 105
Johonnott, Gabriel 40
Justice of the Peace (law book) 1
Justices of the peace 50

Kingfisher (ship) 56

Land Bank 27
Law 1-2, 4, 25, 49, 67, 93
Law books 1-2
Lee, Arthur 68, 87, 104-105
Lee, Richard Henry 105
Leslie, Alexander 43, 56, 92, 96
Letters from a Farmer in Pennsylvania 13
Lexington, Mass. 122
Liberty Tree 35, 38, 39, 88
Littleton, Thomas 1
Lively (ship) 98
Locke, John 5
London 1, 6, 14, 77, 83, 86, 109, 110-111

London (ship) 40, 69
London merchants 30
Lords, House of 10, 106-107
Loring, Joseph Royal 40
Loyal Nine 8

McKean, Thomas 10
Magna Carta 1, 5
Maine 57, 110
Maryland 121
Mass meetings 6, 47, 50, 51, 66, 88-89
Massachusetts agents 6, 7, 17, 68, 78, 79
Massachusetts Bay Colony 1-2, 10, 17, 20, 72, 78, 81, 93
 courts 114
 governors 1-2, 5, 81, 87, 94-96, 102
 government 2, 18, 25, 91-92, 95
 Superior Court 29
Massachusetts charter (1691) 2, 47, 107, 116
Massachusetts Government Act 95, 106-107
Merchants
 American 3-4, 8-9, 10, 12, 13, 19, 34, 38
 association 12, 117, 121
 British 3, 9, 10, 19, 30, 104, 107, 108
Middleborough, Mass. 74
Mifflin, Thomas 43
"Milton" (Hutchinson's estate) 27, 28, 30, 42, 56, 73, 88
Mississippi River 4
Mobs 9, 27, 42, 60, 86, 88-89, 93
Mohawks 60-61
Molyneux, William 40, 66, 91
Monopolies 15, 23, 29, 34, 35, 86
Montagu, John 43, 52, 56, 63

Nancy (ship) 40
Nantucket 51, 72
Natural law 4
Natural rights 2
New England 3, 20, 25, 31, 43, 81
New Hampshire 10

INDEX

New Testament 76
New York (city) 10, 21, 24, 40, 68, 69, 80, 88, 93, 99
   harbor 23
New York Assembly 103
New Yorkers 23
North Carolina 10
North, Frederick (Lord North) 31, 34, 79, 80, 92-94, 103, 104, 108-109, 110, 114-115
   biography 83-86
Northampton, Mass. 72, 115
Nova Scotia 120

Old South Meeting House 47, 50, 52-53, 55, 57, 61
Oliver, Andrew 17, 18, 19, 29, 75, 79
Oliver, Peter (father) 28, 29, 74
Oliver, Peter (son) 28
Oliver family 26, 87
Otis, James 1, 4, 5, 10, 11

Paine, Robert Treat 110
Palmer, William 30
Parliament 3, 4, 6, 14, 19, 20, 30, 31, 34, 49, 83, 85, 117
   authority over colonies 4, 11, 12, 15, 20, 67, 80, 92-94, 109
   colonies petition 9, 10, 14, 106
   members 73, 85
   on tea party 78
   opposition party 106, 108
Pennsylvania 10, 17
Philadelphia 21, 22, 40-41, 43, 68, 69, 77, 80, 88, 99, 100, 109-110, 115
   resolutions against Tea Act 22-23, 38
Philadelphians 23, 41
Phillips, William 66, 101
Pitt, William: *see* Chatham, Earl of
Pitts, John 66
Plural officeholding 25, 28-29
Plymouth, Mass. 74, 95
Polly (ship) 40, 77
Pownall, Thomas 12
Privy Council 19, 78-80, 103, 107

Property 5, 22, 67-68, 83, 89, 94
Punitive acts: *see* Intolerable Acts

Quartering and Mutiny Act 95-96
Quincy, Josiah, Jr. 57, 60, 66

Rainsford Island 42
Raleigh Tavern 100, 105
Reimportation, Law against 42, 49
Resolutions against Tea Act 22-23, 38, 60
Revenue acts 4, 6, 11, 12, 35, 95
Revere, Paul 8, 99, 117
Revolutionary War 2, 89
Rhode Island 10, 26, 114
Richmond, Duke of (Charles Lennox) 106
Rights of the British Colonies Asserted and Proved 5-6
Rights of the people 1-2, 20, 87, 117
   British subjects 11, 120
Riot Act 51
Riots 42, 50, 87-90, 91, 93, 95
Rotch, Francis 40, 50-60, 63
Rotch, Joseph 40
Rowe, John 40, 63, 66, 97
Roxbury, Mass. 44
Royal Exchange Tavern 69
Royal Welch Fusiliers 21
Rutledge, John 115

Salaries of civil officials 11, 20, 29
Salem, Mass. 95, 114
Sanford, Margaret 26
Scollay, John 66
Scott, James 77
Search warrants: *see* "Writs of assistance"
Sedition 114
Seven Years War 3
Sewall, Jonathan 68
Smallpox 42
Smith, John 8
Smuggling 11, 13
Sons of Liberty 8, 21, 39, 41, 43, 88-89
Speke, Anne 83

Stamp Act 6, 12, 27
  opposition 7-9, 10
  rescinded 10-11
Stamp Act Congress 10
Suffolk Resolves 117
Sugar Act 4, 5, 6, 10

Tarring and Feathering Committee 73
Taxes
  in America 4, 7-8, 11, 20, 94
  in Britain 3-4
  power to levy 7-8, 11, 12, 15, 20, 22, 31, 67, 109
  without representation 5, 8, 15
Tea 12, 19, 21, 24, 40, 44, 72
  American market 13, 31
  American reaction to destruction 63, 66-73
  British reaction to destruction 78-81, 83, 87, 91, 104
  compensation discussed 79, 93, 100, 101-102, 104, 108, 110
  consignees 14, 21-24, 30, 33, 35, 38, 39, 40, 41-42, 44, 48, 49, 50-52, 56, 63, 66, 68, 88
  dealers 34, 69
  destroyed tea—value 61, 78
  destruction of tea 61, 87, 89
  laws affecting 49
  nonconsumption 48-49, 61, 69, 72
  price 14-15, 34
  public opinion 73-75
  sales suspended 69, 72
  smuggling 13-15
  see also Boston Tea Party
Tea plan 23, 31, 33-35, 49, 52
Tea Riots: *see* Boston Tea Party
Tea ships 21, 24, 40-42, 47, 52, 55, 61, 69, 88, 89, 92
  watch on 50-52, 92
Tea tax 12-15, 19, 20, 22, 24, 30, 34, 43, 47, 57, 103, 116
Temple, John 18, 72
Thomson, Charles 120
Tories 69, 97, 102, 120

Town House, Boston 47
Townshend Acts 11, 12, 13, 47, 84
Townshend, Charles 11
Townshend duties 13, 17, 19, 23, 24, 34, 52
Trade
  Boston 97-98
  laws 4, 57, 114
  with Britain 9, 99, 104, 120
Treason 67, 91-92, 105
Treaty of Paris 4
Trinity College, Oxford, Eng. 83
Troops: *see* British troops; Quartering and Mutiny Act
Trott, George 8
Tryon, William 24, 93

Violence 88-90, 106, 115
Virginia 7, 10, 20, 100, 116
  resolutions 7-8, 10
Voting qualifications in Massachusetts 2

Waldershare, Kent, Eng. 85
Walpole, Horace 14, 81, 107
Walpole, Robert 14
Ward, Henry 10
Warren, James 35, 67
Warren, Joseph 8, 40, 66, 91, 99
Warren, Mercy Otis 89
Washington, George 116
Watson, George 74
Watson, Polly 74
Wedderburn, Alexander 78-79, 91
Welles, Henry 8
West Indies 3, 98, 120
Whately, William 18, 72
Whigs 69, 97
Wilkes, John 86
William III 85
William (ship) 40, 138
Williams, Jonathan 91
Williamsburg, Va. 100
Williamson, Hugh 68
Winslow, Joshua 40
Winthrop, John 1, 15
"Writs of assistance" 11

Young, Thomas 60-61, 66, 91, 99